to

_____

100 DEVOTIONALS
for guys

Cover Design by Kim Russell / Wahoo Designs
Page Layout by Bart Dawson

ISBN 1-58334-318-0

ISBN-13 978-1-58334-318-0

2 minutes
A DAY

100 DEVOTIONALS
for guys

Introduction

Okay, it's a fact: you're a very busy guy. But here's a question: can you squeeze two little minutes into your hectic schedule? If you're smart, the answer will be a resounding yes. Why? Because the two minutes in question are the minutes that you give to God!

God has a plan for everything, and that includes you. But figuring out that plan may not be easy. That's why you need to talk to God . . . a lot. The more you talk to your Creator, the sooner He will help you figure out exactly what plans He has in store for you. So do yourself a favor: start talking to Him now. As you begin that conversation, this little book can help.

This book contains 100 short devotional readings of particular interest to guys who, like you, are very busy. Each chapter contains a Bible verse, a brief devotional reading, quotations from noted Christian men (plus quotes from a few women tossed in for good measure), and a prayer.

Would you like to have a life that's above and beyond the ordinary? Talk to God about it. Do you have questions that you can't answer? God has answers. Are you seeking to improve some aspect of your life? The Bible is the greatest self-improvement book of all time. Do you want to be a better person and a better Christian? If so, ask for God's help and ask for it many times each day . . . starting with a regular, heartfelt morning devotional. Even two minutes is enough time to change your day . . . and your life.

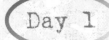

Who's First?

*The thing you should want most is God's kingdom
and doing what God wants. Then all these other things
you need will be given to you.*

MATTHEW 6:33 NCV

Who is in charge of your heart? Is it God, or is it something else? Have you given Christ your heart, your soul, your talents, your time, and your testimony? Or are you giving Him little more than a few hours each Sunday morning?

In the book of Exodus, God warns that we should place no gods before Him. Yet all too often, we place our Lord in second, third, or fourth place as we worship other things. When we unwittingly place possessions or relationships above our love for the Creator, we create big problems for ourselves.

Does God rule your heart? Make certain that the honest answer to this question is a resounding yes. In the life of every radical believer, God comes first. And that's precisely the place that He deserves in your heart.

more stuff to think about

God is able to do anything He pleases with one ordinary person fully consecrated to Him.

HENRY BLACKABY AND CLAUDE KING

We become whatever we are committed to.

RICK WARREN

Today's Prayer

Dear Lord, today I will honor You with my thoughts, my actions, and my prayers. I will seek to please You, and I will strive to serve You. Your blessings are as limitless as Your love. And because I have been so richly blessed, I will worship You, Father, with thanksgiving in my heart and praise on my lips, this day and forever. Amen

for guys

It's a Wonderful Life

*For whoever finds me finds life and receives
favor from the LORD.*
PROVERBS 8:35 NIV

Life can be tough sometimes, but it's also wonderful—
and it's a glorious gift from God. How will you use that
gift? Every day, including this one, comes gift-wrapped
from God—your job is to unwrap that gift, to use it wisely,
and to give thanks to the Giver.

Instead of sleepwalking through life, you must wake
up and live in the precious present. Each waking moment
holds the potential to celebrate, to serve, to share, or to
love. Because you are a person with incalculable potential,
each moment has incalculable value. Your challenge is
to experience each day to the full as you seek to live in
accordance with God's plan for your life. When you do,
you'll experience His abundance and His peace.

Are you willing to treat this day (and every one hereafter)
as a special gift to be savored and celebrated? You should—
and if you seek to Live with a capital L, you most certainly
will.

more stuff to think about

Life is a glorious opportunity.

BILLY GRAHAM

People, places, and things were never meant to give us life.
God alone is the author of a fulfilling life.

GARY SMALLEY & JOHN TRENT

Today's Prayer

Dear Lord, You have created this glorious universe, and You have created me. Let me live my life to the fullest, and let me use my life for Your glory, today and every day. Amen

Problem-solving 101

People who do what is right may have many problems,
but the Lord will solve them all.
PSALM 34:19 NCV

Life is an adventure in problem-solving. When it comes to solving the problems of everyday living, we often know precisely what needs to be done, but we may be slow in doing it—especially if what needs to be done is difficult. So we put off till tomorrow what should be done today.

As a young man living here in the 21st-century, you have your own set of challenges. As you face those challenges, you may be comforted by this fact: Trouble, of every kind, is temporary. Yet God's grace is eternal. And worries, of every kind, are temporary. But God's love is everlasting. The troubles that concern you will pass. God remains. And for every problem, God has a solution.

The words of Psalm 34 remind us that the Lord solves problems for "people who do what is right." And usually, doing "what is right" means doing the uncomfortable work of confronting our problems sooner rather than later. So with no further ado, let the problem-solving begin . . . right now.

more stuff to think about

Each problem is a God-appointed instructor.

CHARLES SWINDOLL

Life will be made or broken at the place where we meet and deal with obstacles.

E. STANLEY JONES

Today's Prayer

Lord, sometimes my problems are simply too big for me, but they are never too big for You. Let me turn my troubles over to You, Lord, and let me trust in You today and for all eternity. Amen

for guys

Critics Beware

Don't speak evil against each other, my dear brothers and sisters. If you criticize each other and condemn each other, then you are criticizing and condemning God's law. But you are not a judge who can decide whether the law is right or wrong. Your job is to obey it.

JAMES 4:11 NLT

From experience, we know that it is easier to criticize than to correct. And we know that it is easier to find faults than solutions. Yet the urge to criticize others remains a powerful temptation for most of us. Our task, as obedient believers, is to break the twin habits of negative thinking and critical speech.

Negativity is highly contagious: we give it to others who, in turn, give it back to us. This cycle can be broken by positive thoughts, heartfelt prayers, and encouraging words. As thoughtful servants of a loving God, we can use the transforming power of Christ's love to break the chains of negativity. And we should.

more stuff to think about

We shall never come to the perfect man
til we come to the perfect world.

MATTHEW HENRY

The scrutiny we give other people should be for ourselves.

OSWALD CHAMBERS

Today's Prayer

Help me, Lord, rise above the need to criticize others.
May my own shortcomings humble me, and may I
always be a source of genuine encouragement to my
family and friends. Amen

for guys

So Many Questions

We are pressured in every way but not crushed;
we are perplexed but not in despair.

2 CORINTHIANS 4:8 HCSB

So many questions and so few answers! If that statement seems to describe the current state of your spiritual life, don't panic. Even the most faithful Christians are overcome by occasional bouts of fear and doubt. You are no different.

When you feel that your faith is being tested to its limits, seek the comfort and assurance of the One who sent His Son as a sacrifice for you. And remember: Even when you feel very distant from God, God is never distant from you. When you sincerely seek His presence, He will touch your heart, calm your fears, and restore your soul.

more stuff to think about

A prudent question is one-half of wisdom.

FRANCIS BACON

Be to the world a sign that while we as Christians
do not have all the answers, we do know
and care about the questions.

BILLY GRAHAM

Today's Prayer

Dear Lord, when I have questions that I can't answer,
I will trust You. And I will do my best to offer help to
those who need it, so that through me, others, too, might
come to know You and trust You. Amen

for guys

The Right Kind of Fear

*A simple life in the Fear-of-God is better than
a rich life with a ton of headaches.*
PROVERBS 15:16 MSG

God's hand shapes the universe, and it shapes our lives. God maintains absolute sovereignty over His creation, and His power is beyond comprehension. As believers, we must cultivate a sincere respect for God's awesome power. God has dominion over all things, and until we acknowledge His sovereignty, we lack the humility we need to live righteously, and we lack the humility we need to become wise.

The fear of the Lord is, indeed, the beginning of knowledge. So today, as you face the realities of everyday life, remember this: until you acquire a healthy, respectful fear of God's power, your education is incomplete, and so is your faith.

more stuff to think about

A healthy fear of God will do much to deter us from sin.

CHARLES SWINDOLL

The remarkable thing about fearing God is that
when you fear God, you fear nothing else,
whereas if you do not fear God, you fear everything else.

OSWALD CHAMBERS

Today's Prayer

Lord, You love me and protect me. I praise You, Father,
for Your grace, and I respect You for Your infinite
power. Let my greatest fear in life be the fear of
displeasing You. Amen

for guys

Answering the Call

God chose you to be his people, so I urge you now
to live the life to which God called you.

EPHESIANS 4:1 NCV

It is vitally important that you heed God's call. In John 15:
16, Jesus says, "You did not choose me, but I chose you
and appointed you to go and bear fruit—fruit that will
last" (NIV). In other words, you have been called by Christ,
and now, it is up to you to decide precisely how you will
answer.

Have you already found your special calling? If so,
you're a very lucky guy. If not, keep searching and keep
praying until you discover it. And remember this: God has
important work for you to do—work that no one else on
earth can accomplish but you.

more stuff to think about

When you become consumed by God's call on your life,
everything will take on new meaning and significance.
You will begin to see every facet of your life,
including your pain, as a means through which God
can work to bring others to Himself.

CHARLES STANLEY

If God has called you, do not spend time
looking over your shoulder to see who is following you.

CORRIE TEN BOOM

Today's Prayer

Heavenly Father, You have called me, and I
acknowledge that calling. In these quiet moments
before this busy day unfolds, I come to You. I will
study Your Word and seek Your guidance. Give me the
wisdom to know Your will for my life and the courage
to follow wherever You may lead me, today and forever.
Amen

for guys

God's Promises

Let's keep a firm grip on the promises that keep us going.
He always keeps his word.
HEBREWS 10:23 MSG

God has made quite a few promises to you, and He intends to keep every single one of them. You will find these promises in a book like no other: the Holy Bible. The Bible is your roadmap for life here on earth and for life eternal. As a believer, you are called upon to trust its promises, to follow its commandments, and to share its Good News.

God has made promises to all of humanity and to you. God's promises never fail and they never grow old. You must trust those promises and share them with your family, with your friends, and with the world . . . starting now . . . and ending never.

more stuff to think about

God's promises are overflowings from his great heart.

C. H. SPURGEON

The stars may fall, but God's promises will stand
and be fulfilled.

J. I. PACKER

Today's Prayer

Lord, Your Holy Word contains promises, and I will
trust them. I will use the Bible as my guide, and I will
trust You, Lord, to speak to me through Your Holy
Spirit and through Your Holy Word, this day and
forever. Amen

for guys

Talking Behind Their Backs

If anyone considers himself religious and yet does not keep a tight rein on his tongue, he deceives himself and his religion is worthless.

JAMES 1:26 NIV

ace it: gossip is bad—and the Bible clearly tells us that gossip is wrong.

When we say things that we don't want other people to know we said, we're being somewhat dishonest, but if the things we say aren't true, we're being very dishonest. Either way, we have done something that we may regret later, especially when the other person finds out.

So do yourself a big favor: don't gossip. It's a waste of words, and it's the wrong thing to do. You'll feel better about yourself if you don't gossip (and other people will feel better about you, too). So don't do it!

more stuff to think about

Change the heart, and you change the speech.
WARREN WIERSBE

The great test of a man's character is his tongue.
OSWALD CHAMBERS

Today's Prayer

Lord, You have warned me that I will be judged by the words I speak. And, You have commanded me to choose my words carefully so that I might be a source of encouragement and hope to my family and to the world. Let the words that I speak today be worthy of the One who has saved me forever. Amen

for guys

He's Here

I am not alone, because the Father is with Me.
JOHN 16:32 HCSB

Do you ever wonder if God really hears your prayers? If so, you're in good company: lots of very faithful Christians have wondered the same thing. In fact, some of the biggest heroes in the Bible had their doubts—and so, perhaps, will you. But when you have your doubts, remember this: God isn't on vacation, and He hasn't moved out of town. God isn't taking a coffee break, and He isn't snoozing on the couch. He's right here, right now, listening to your thoughts and prayers, watching over your every move.

As the demands of everyday life weigh down upon you, you may be tempted to ignore God's presence or—worse yet—to rebel against His commandments. But, when you quiet yourself and acknowledge His presence, God touches your heart and restores your spirit. So why not let Him do it right now?

more stuff to think about

Get yourself into the presence of the loving Father.
Just place yourself before Him, and look up into, His face;
think of His love, His wonderful, tender, pitying love.

ANDREW MURRAY

There is a basic urge: the longing for unity.
You desire a reunion with God—with God your Father.

E. STANLEY JONES

Today's Prayer

Dear Lord, You are with me always. Help me feel Your
presence in every situation and every circumstance.
Today, Dear God, let me feel You and acknowledge
Your presence, Your love, and Your Son. Amen

for guys

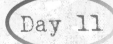
A Rule That's Golden

Do to others as you would have them do to you.
LUKE 6:31 NIV

Is the Golden Rule your rule, or is it just another Bible verse that goes in one ear and out the other? Jesus made Himself perfectly clear: He instructed you to treat other people in the same way that you want to be treated. But sometimes, especially when you're feeling pressure from friends, or when you're tired or upset, obeying the Golden Rule can seem like an impossible task—but it's not.

God wants each of us to treat other people with respect, kindness, and courtesy. He wants us to rise above our own imperfections, and He wants us to treat others with unselfishness and love. To make it short and sweet, God wants us to obey the Golden Rule, and He knows we can do it.

So if you're wondering how to treat someone else, ask the person you see every time you look into the mirror. The answer you receive will tell you exactly what to do.

more stuff to think about

Faith never asks whether good works are to be done,
but has done them before there is time to ask the question,
and it is always doing them.

MARTIN LUTHER

When you extend hospitality to others, you're not trying to
impress people, you're trying to reflect God to them.

MAX LUCADO

Today's Prayer

Dear Lord, Your Golden Rule is a perfect standard
to use with my friends and neighbors. Enable me to
respect others as I want them to respect me. Help me to
walk in their shoes and to see life from their perspective.
Help me, Father, to be a nurturing, loving person every
day that I live, and may the glory be yours. Amen

for guys

Time for Fun

So I recommend having fun, because there is nothing better for people to do in this world than to eat, drink, and enjoy life. That way they will experience some happiness along with all the hard work God gives them.

ECCLESIASTES 8:15 NLT

Are you a guy who takes time each day to really enjoy life? Hopefully so. After all, you are the recipient of a precious gift—the gift of life. And because God has seen fit to give you this gift, it is incumbent upon you to use it and to enjoy it. But sometimes, amid the inevitable pressures of everyday living, really enjoying life may seem almost impossible. It is not.

For most of us, fun is as much a function of attitude as it is a function of environment. So whether you're standing victorious atop one of life's mountains or trudging through one of life's valleys, enjoy yourself. You deserve to have fun today, and God wants you to have fun today . . . so what on earth are you waiting for?

more stuff to think about

The happiest people in the world are not those who have no problems, but the people who have learned to live with those things that are less than perfect.

JAMES DOBSON

If we don't hunger and thirst after righteousness, we'll become anemic and feel miserable in our Christian experience.

FRANKLIN GRAHAM

Today's Prayer

Dear Lord, You are my strength and my joy. I will rejoice in the day that You have made, and I will give thanks for the countless blessings that You have given me. Let me be a joyful Christian, Father, as I share the Good News of Your Son, and let me praise You for all the marvelous things You have done. Amen

for guys

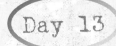

A Happy Christian

How happy are those who can live in your house,
always singing your praises. How happy are those
who are strong in the Lord....

PSALM 84:4-5 NLT

Happiness depends less upon our circumstances than upon our thoughts. When we turn our thoughts to God, to His gifts, and to His glorious creation, we experience the joy that God intends for His children. But, when we focus on the negative aspects of life, we suffer needlessly.

Do you sincerely want to be a happy Christian? Then set your mind and your heart upon God's love and His grace. The fullness of life in Christ is available to all who seek it and claim it. Count yourself among that number. Seek first the salvation that is available through a personal relationship with Jesus Christ, and then claim the joy, the peace, and the spiritual abundance that the Shepherd offers His sheep.

more stuff to think about

Whoever possesses God is happy.

St. Augustine

There is no correlation between wealth and happiness.

Larry Burkett

Today's Prayer

Lord, make me a happy Christian. Let me rejoice in the gift of this day, and let me praise You for the gift of Your Son. Make me be a joyful teacher, Lord, as I share Your Good News with all those who need Your healing touch. Amen

for guys

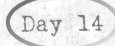

What a Friend

Therefore if any man be in Christ, he is a new creature:
old things are passed away;
behold, all things are become new.

2 CORINTHIANS 5:17 KJV

Our circumstances change but Jesus does not. Even when the world seems to be trembling between our feet, Jesus remains the spiritual bedrock that cannot be moved.

The old familiar hymn begins, "What a friend we have in Jesus...." No truer words were ever penned. Jesus is the sovereign friend and ultimate Savior of mankind. Christ showed enduring love for His believers by willingly sacrificing His own life so that we might have eternal life. Let us love Him, praise Him, and share His message of salvation with our neighbors and with the world.

more stuff to think about

Jesus was the perfect reflection of God's nature
in every situation He encountered during
His time here on earth.

BILL HYBELS

Jesus: the proof of God's love.

PHILIP YANCEY

Today's Prayer

Heavenly Father, I praise You for Your Son. Jesus is my
Savior and my strength. Let me share His Good News
with all who cross my path, and let me share His love
with all who need His healing touch. Amen

for guys

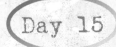

Obedience Now

*Not everyone who says to me, "Lord, Lord," will enter
the kingdom of heaven, but only he who does
the will of my Father who is in heaven.*

MATTHEW 7:21 NIV

God's commandments are not "suggestions," and they are not "helpful hints." They are, instead, immutable laws which, if followed, lead to repentance, salvation, and abundance. But if you choose to disobey the commandments of your Heavenly Father or the teachings of His Son, you will most surely reap a harvest of regret.

The formula for a successful life is surprisingly straightforward: Study God's Word and obey it. Does this sound too simple? Perhaps it is simple, but it is also the only way to reap the marvelous riches that God has in store for you.

more stuff to think about

Obedience is the outward expression of your love of God.

HENRY BLACKABY

All true knowledge of God is born out of obedience.

JOHN CALVIN

Today's Prayer

Heavenly Father, when I turn my thoughts away from You and Your Word, I suffer. But when I obey Your commandments, when I place my faith in You, I am secure. Let me live according to Your commandments. Direct my path far from the temptations and distractions of this world. And, let me discover Your will and follow it, Dear Lord, this day and always. Amen

for guys

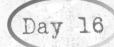
You and Your Family

...these should learn first of all to put their religion into practice by caring for their own family....

1 TIMOTHY 5:4 NIV

A loving family is a treasure from God. If God has blessed you with a close knit, supportive clan, offer a word of thanks to your Creator because He has given you one of His most precious earthy possessions. Your obligation, in response to God's gift, is to treat your family in ways that are consistent with His commandments.

You live in a fast-paced, demanding world, a place where life can be difficult and pressures can be intense. As those pressures build, you may tend to focus so intently upon your obligations that you lose sight, albeit temporarily, of your spiritual and emotional needs (that's one reason why a regular daily devotional time is so important; it offers a badly-needed dose of perspective).

So the next time your family life becomes a little stressful, remember this: That little band of men, women, kids, and babies is a priceless treasure on temporary loan from the Father above. And it's your responsibility to praise God for that gift—and to act accordingly.

2 minutes A DAY

more stuff to think about

The only true source of meaning in life is found in love for God and his son Jesus Christ, and love for mankind, beginning with our own families.

JAMES DOBSON

Never give your family the leftovers and crumbs of your time.

CHARLES SWINDOLL

Today's Prayer

Dear Lord, I am part of Your family, and I praise You for Your gifts and Your love. Father, You have also blessed me with my earthly family. Let me show love and acceptance for my own family so that through me, they might come to know You. Amen

for guys

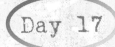

Sharing Your Faith

But respect Christ as the holy Lord in your hearts.
Always be ready to answer everyone who asks you
to explain about the hope you have.

1 Peter 3:15 NCV

A good way to build your faith is by talking about it—and that's precisely what God wants you to do. In his second letter to Timothy, Paul shares a message to believers of every generation when he writes, "God has not given us a spirit of timidity" (1:7). Paul's meaning is clear: When sharing your testimony, you must be courageous and unashamed.

Let's face facts: You live in a world that desperately needs the healing message of Jesus Christ. Every believer, including you, bears responsibility for sharing the Good News. And it is important to remember that your give your testimony through your words and your actions.

So today, preach the Gospel through your words and your deeds…but not necessarily in that order.

more stuff to think about

To stand in an uncaring world and say,
"See, here is the Christ" is a daring act of courage.

CALVIN MILLER

To take up the cross means that you take your stand
for the Lord Jesus no matter what it costs.

BILLY GRAHAM

Today's Prayer

Dear Lord, You sent Your Son Jesus to die on a cross for me. Jesus endured indignity, suffering, and death so that I might live. Because He lives, I, too, have Your promise of eternal life. Let me share this Good News, Lord, with a world that so desperately needs Your healing hand and the salvation of Your Son. Today, let me share the message of Jesus Christ through my words and my deeds. Amen

for guys

The Wisdom to be Humble

God has chosen you and made you his holy people.
He loves you. So always do these things:
Show mercy to others, be kind, humble, gentle, and patient.
COLOSSIANS 3:12 NCV

Humility is not, in most cases, a naturally occurring human trait. Most of us, it seems, are more than willing to overestimate our own accomplishments. We are tempted to say, "Look how wonderful I am!" . . . hoping all the while that the world will agree with our own self-appraisals. But those of us who fall prey to the sin of pride should beware—God is definitely not impressed by our prideful proclamations.

God honors humility . . . and He rewards those who humbly serve Him. So if you've acquired the wisdom to be humble, then you are to be congratulated. But if you've not yet overcome the tendency to overestimate your own accomplishments, then God still has some important (and perhaps painful) lessons to teach you—lessons about humility that you still need to learn.

more stuff to think about

Humility is not thinking less of yourself;
it is thinking of yourself less.

RICK WARREN

It was pride that changed angels into devils;
it is humility that makes men as angels.

ST. AUGUSTINE

Today's Prayer

Heavenly Father, Jesus clothed Himself with humility when He chose to leave heaven and come to earth to live and die for us, His children. Christ is my Master and my example. Clothe me with humility, Lord, so that I might be more like Your Son, and keep me mindful that You are the giver and sustainer of life, and to You, Dear Lord, goes the glory and the praise. Amen

for guys

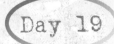

Watching the Donut

I can do everything through him that gives me strength.
PHILIPPIANS 4:13 NIV

On the wall of a little donut shop, the sign said: As you travel through life, brother, Whatever be your goal, Keep your eye upon the donut, And not upon the hole.

Are you a Christian who keeps your eye upon the donut, or have you acquired the bad habit of looking only at the hole? Hopefully, you spend most of your waking hours looking at the donut (and thanking God for it).

Christianity and pessimism don't mix. So do yourself a favor: choose to be a hope-filled Christian. Think optimistically about your life and your future. Trust your hopes, not your fears. Take time to celebrate God's glorious creation. And then, when you've filled your heart with hope and gladness, share your optimism with your friends. They'll be better for it, and so will you. But not necessarily in that order.

more stuff to think about

Keep your feet on the ground, but let your heart soar
as high as it will. Refuse to be average or to surrender
to the chill of your spiritual environment.

A. W. TOZER

The people whom I have seen succeed best in life have
always been cheerful and hopeful people who went about
their business with a smile on their faces.

CHARLES KINGSLEY

Today's Prayer

Lord, let me be an expectant Christian. Let me expect the
best from You, and let me look for the best in others. If
I become discouraged, Father, turn my thoughts and
my prayers to You. Let me trust You, Lord, to direct
my life. And, let me share my faith and optimism with
others, today and every day that I live. Amen

for guys

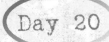

Peer Pressure 101

We must obey God rather than men.
ACTS 5:29 HCSB

Rick Warren observed, "Those who follow the crowd usually get lost in it." We know those words to be true, but oftentimes we fail to live by them. Instead of trusting God for guidance, we imitate our friends and suffer the consequences. Instead of seeking to please our Father in heaven, we strive to please our peers, with decidedly mixed results. Instead of doing the right thing, we do the "easy" thing or the "popular" thing. And when we do, we pay a high price for our shortsightedness.

Would you like a time-tested formula for successful living? Here is a simple formula that is proven and true: don't give in to peer pressure. Period.

Instead of getting lost in the crowd, you should find guidance from God. Does this sound too simple? Perhaps it is simple, but it is also the only way to reap all the marvelous riches that God has in store for you.

more stuff to think about

Do you want to be wise? Choose wise friends.

CHARLES SWINDOLL

Those who follow the crowd usually get lost in it.

RICK WARREN

Today's Prayer

Dear Lord, other people may encourage me to stray from Your path, but I wish to follow in the footsteps of Your Son. Give me the vision to see the right path—and the wisdom to follow it—today and every day of my life. Amen

for guys

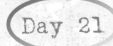

Fitness Matters

Whatever you eat or drink or whatever you do,
you must do all for the glory of God.

1 CORINTHIANS 10:31 NLT

Are you shaping up or spreading out? Do you eat sensibly and exercise regularly, or do you spend most of your time on the couch with a Twinkie in one hand and a clicker in the other? Are you choosing to treat your body like a temple or a trash heap? How you answer these questions will help determine how long you live and how well you live.

Physical fitness is a choice, a choice that requires discipline—it's as simple as that. So, do yourself this favor: treat your body like a one-of-a-kind gift from God . . . because that's precisely what your body is.

more stuff to think about

A Christian should no more defile his body than
a Jew would defile the temple.

WARREN WIERSBE

If you desire to improve your physical well-being and
your emotional outlook, increasing your faith can help you.

JOHN MAXWELL

Today's Prayer

Dear Lord, my body is Your temple—I will treat it with
care. Amen

for guys

Stand Up and Be Counted

*Do what God's teaching says; when you only listen
and do nothing, you are fooling yourselves.*
JAMES 1:22 NCV

Face facts: this world is inhabited by quite a few people who are very determined to do bad things. The devil and his human helpers are working 24/7 to cause pain and heartbreak in every corner of the globe . . . including your corner. So you'd better beware.

Your job, if you choose to accept it, is to recognize bad behavior and fight it. How? By standing up for your beliefs, that's how!

The moment that you decide to fight mischief whenever you see it, you can no longer be a lukewarm, halfhearted Christian. And, when you are no longer a lukewarm Christian, God rejoices (and the devil doesn't).

So stand up for your beliefs. And remember this: in the battle of good versus evil, the devil never takes a day off . . . and neither should you.

more stuff to think about

God calls us to be committed to Him, to be committed to
making a difference, and to be committed to reconciliation.

BILL HYBELS

Once you have thoroughly examined your values and
articulated them, you will be able to steer you life by them.

JOHN MAXWELL

Today's Prayer

Heavenly Father, I believe in You, and I believe in Your
Word. Help me to live in such a way that my actions
validate my beliefs—and let the glory be Yours forever.
Amen

for guys

Real Repentance

If you hide your sins, you will not succeed.
If you confess and reject them, you will receive mercy.

PROVERBS 28:13 NCV

W ho among us has sinned? All of us. But, God calls upon us to turn away from sin by following His commandments. And the good news is this: When we do ask God's forgiveness and turn our hearts to Him, He forgives us absolutely and completely.

Genuine repentance requires more than simply offering God apologies for our misdeeds. Real repentance may start with feelings of sorrow and remorse, but it ends only when we turn away from the sin that has heretofore distanced us from our Creator. In truth, we offer our most meaningful apologies to God, not with our words, but with our actions. As long as we are still engaged in sin, we may be "repenting," but we have not fully "repented."

Is there an aspect of your life that is distancing you from your God? If so, ask for His forgiveness, and—just as importantly—stop sinning. Then, wrap yourself in the protection of God's Word. When you do, you will be secure.

more stuff to think about

Ten thousand confessions, if they do not spring from really contrite hearts, shall only be additions to their guilt.

C. H. SPURGEON

Repentance begins with confession of our guilt and recognition that our sin is against God.

CHARLES STANLEY

Today's Prayer

When I stray from Your commandments, Lord, I must not only confess my sins, I must also turn from them. When I fall short, help me to change. When I reject Your Word and Your will for my life, guide me back to Your side. Forgive my sins, Dear Lord, and help me live according to Your plan for my life. Your plan is perfect, Father; I am not. Let me trust in You. Amen

for guys

Time for God

Don't burn out; keep yourselves fueled and aflame.
Be alert servants of the Master, cheerfully expectant.
Don't quit in hard times; pray all the harder.

ROMANS 12:11-12 MSG

Are you making time each day to praise God and to study His Word? If so, you know firsthand the blessings that He offers those who worship Him consistently and sincerely. But, if you have unintentionally allowed the hustle and bustle of your busy day to come between you and your Creator, then you must slow down, take a deep breath, and rearrange your priorities.

God loved this world so much that He sent His Son to save it. And now only one real question remains for you: what will you do in response to God's love? The answer should be obvious: God must come first in your life. He is the Giver of all good things, and He is the One who sent His Son so that you might have eternal life. He deserves your prayers, your obedience, your stewardship, and your love—and He deserves these things all day every day, not just on Sunday mornings.

more stuff to think about

This is a day when we are so busy doing everything
that we have no time to be anything. Even religiously
we are so occupied with activities that
we have no time to know God.

VANCE HAVNER

Busyness is the great enemy of relationships.

RICK WARREN

Today's Prayer

Dear Lord, sometimes, I am distracted by the busyness
of the day or the demands of the moment. When I am
worried or anxious, Father, turn my thoughts back
to You. Help me to trust Your will, to follow Your
commands, and to accept Your peace, today and forever.
Amen

for guys

Your Own Worst Critic?

Those who wait for perfect weather will never plant seeds;
those who look at every cloud will never harvest crops.
Plant early in the morning, and work until evening,
because you don't know if this or that will succeed.
They might both do well.

ECCLESIASTES 11:4,6 NCV

When God made you, he equipped you with an array of talents and abilities that are uniquely yours. It's up to you to discover those talents and to use them, but sometimes your own perfectionism may get in the way.

If you're your own worst critic, give it up. After all, God doesn't expect you to be perfect, and if that's okay with Him, then it should be okay with you, too.

When you accepted Christ as your Savior, God accepted you for all eternity. Now, it's your turn to accept yourself. When you do, you'll feel a tremendous weight being lifted from your shoulders. And that's as it should be. After all, only one earthly being ever lived life to perfection, and He was the Son of God. The rest of us have fallen short of God's standard and need to be accepting of our own limitations as well as the limitations of others.

more stuff to think about

What makes a Christian a Christian is not perfection
but forgiveness.

MAX LUCADO

The happiest people in the world are not those
who have no problems, but the people who have learned to
live with those things that are less than perfect.

JAMES DOBSON

Today's Prayer

Lord, this world has so many expectations of me, but today I will not seek to meet the world's expectations; I will do my best to meet Your expectations. I will make You my ultimate priority, Lord, by serving You, by praising You, by loving You, and by obeying You. Amen

for guys

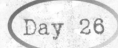

The Ultimate Armor

If God is for us, who can be against us?
ROMANS 8:31 NIV

G od has promised to protect us, and He intends to keep His promise. In a world filled with dangers and temptations, God is the ultimate armor. In a world filled with misleading messages, God's Word is the ultimate truth. In a world filled with more frustrations than we can count, God's Son offers the ultimate peace.

Will you accept God's peace and wear God's armor against the dangers of our world? Hopefully so—because when you do, you can live courageously, knowing that you possess the ultimate protection: God's unfailing love for you.

more stuff to think about

Under heaven's lock and key, we are protected by
the most efficient security system available:
the power of God.

CHARLES SWINDOLL

The Rock of Ages is the great sheltering encirclement.

OSWALD CHAMBERS

Today's Prayer

Lord, sometimes life is difficult. Sometimes, I am
worried, weary, or heartbroken. And sometimes, I
encounter powerful temptations to disobey Your
commandments. But, when I lift my eyes to You,
Father, You strengthen me. When I am weak, You lift
me up. Today, I will turn to You for strength, for hope,
for direction, and for deliverance. Amen

for guys

Do You Believe in Miracles?

You are the God who performs miracles;
you display your power among the peoples.

PSALM 77:14 NIV

D o you believe that God is at work in the world? And do you also believe that nothing is impossible for Him? If so, then you also believe that God is perfectly capable of doing things that you, as a mere human being with limited vision and limited understanding, would deem to be utterly impossible. And that's precisely what God does.

Since the moment that He created our universe out of nothingness, God has made a habit of doing miraculous things. And He still works miracles today. Expect Him to work miracles in your own life, and then be watchful. With God, absolutely nothing is impossible, including an amazing assortment of miracles that He stands ready, willing, and able to perform for you and yours.

more stuff to think about

Too many Christians live below the miracle level.

VANCE HAVNER

Only God can move mountains,
but faith and prayer can move God.

E. M. BOUNDS

Today's Prayer

Lord, for You, nothing is impossible. Let me trust in Your power to do the miraculous, and let me trust in Your willingness to work miracles in my life—and in my heart. Amen

for guys

Listen Carefully

The one who is from God listens to God's words.
This is why you don't listen, because you are not from God.
JOHN 8:47 HCSB

Sometimes God speaks loudly and clearly. More often, He speaks in a quiet voice—and if you are wise, you will be listening carefully when He does. To do so, you must carve out quiet moments each day to study His Word and sense His direction.

Can you quiet yourself long enough to listen to your conscience? Are you attuned to the subtle guidance of your intuition? Are you willing to pray sincerely and then to wait quietly for God's response? Hopefully so. Usually God refrains from sending His messages on stone tablets or city billboards. More often, He communicates in subtler ways. If you sincerely desire to hear His voice, you must listen carefully, and you must do so in the silent corners of your quiet, willing heart.

more stuff to think about

Listening is loving.

ZIG ZIGLAR

In the soul-searching of our lives,
we are to stay quiet so we can hear Him say
all that He wants to say to us in our hearts.

CHARLES SWINDOLL

Today's Prayer

Lord, give me the wisdom to be a good listener. Help me listen carefully to my family, to my friends, and—most importantly—to You. Amen

for guys

Big Plans

"I say this because I know what I am planning for you,"
says the Lord. "I have good plans for you, not plans to hurt
you. I will give you hope and a good future."

JEREMIAH 29:11 NCV

D o you think that God has big plans for you, or do think that God wants you to be a do-nothing Christian? The answer should be obvious, but just for the record, here are the facts: 1. God has plans for your life that are far grander than you can imagine. 2. It's up to you to discover those plans and accomplish them . . . or not.

The most important decision of your life is, of course, your commitment to accept Jesus Christ as your personal Lord and Savior. And once your eternal destiny is secured, you will undoubtedly ask yourself "What now, Lord?" If you earnestly seek God's plan for your life, you will find it…in time.

Sometimes, God's plans are crystal clear, but other times, He may lead you through the wilderness before He delivers you to the Promised Land. So be patient, keep praying, and keep seeking His will for your life. When you do, you'll be amazed at the marvelous things that an all-powerful, all-knowing God can do.

more stuff to think about

One of the wonderful things about being a Christian is
the knowledge that God has a plan for our lives.

WARREN WIERSBE

Faith never knows where it is being led,
but it loves the One who is leading.

OSWALD CHAMBERS

Today's Prayer

Dear Lord, I will seek Your plan for my life. Even when
I don't understand why things happen, I will trust You.
Even when I am uncertain of my next step, I will trust
You. There are many things that I cannot do, Lord, and
there are many things that I cannot understand. But
one thing I can do is to trust You always. And I will.
Amen

for guys

So Laugh!

*Laugh with your happy friends when they're happy;
share tears when they're down.*
ROMANS 12:15 MSG

Laughter is a gift from God, a gift that He intends for us to use. Yet sometimes, because of the inevitable stresses of everyday living, we fail to find the fun in life. When we allow life's inevitable disappointments to cast a pall over our lives and our souls, we do a profound disservice to ourselves and to our loved ones.

If you've allowed the clouds of life to obscure the blessings of life, perhaps you've formed the unfortunate habit of taking things just a little too seriously. If so, it's time to fret a little less and laugh a little more.

So today, look for the humor that most certainly surrounds you—when you do, you'll find it. And remember: God created laughter for a reason...and Father indeed knows best. So laugh!

more stuff to think about

If you want people to feel comfortable around you,
to enjoy being with you, then learn to laugh at yourself
and find humor in life's little mishaps.

DENNIS SWANBERG

Laughter is like premium gasoline:
It takes the knock out of living.

ANONYMOUS

Today's Prayer

Lord, when I begin to take myself or my life too
seriously, let me laugh. When I rush from place to place,
slow me down, Lord, and let me laugh. Put a smile on
my face, Dear Lord, and let me share that smile with all
who cross my path . . . and let me laugh. Amen

for guys

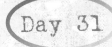

Let God Judge

Stop judging others, and you will not be judged.
Stop criticizing others, or it will all come back on you.
If you forgive others, you will be forgiven.

LUKE 6:37 NLT

Here's something worth thinking about: If you judge other people harshly, God will judge you in the same fashion. But that's not all (thank goodness!). The Bible also promises that if you forgive others, you, too, will be forgiven. Have you developed the bad habit of behaving yourself like an amateur judge and jury, assigning blame and condemnation wherever you go? If so, it's time to grow up and obey God. When it comes to judging everything and everybody, God doesn't need your help . . . and He doesn't want it.

2 minutes A DAY

more stuff to think about

Christians think they are prosecuting attorneys
or judges, when, in reality, God has called
all of us to be witnesses.

WARREN WIERSBE

Don't judge other people more harshly than
you want God to judge you.

MARIE T. FREEMAN

Today's Prayer

Dear Lord, sometimes I am quick to judge others.
But, You have commanded me not to judge. Keep me
mindful, Father, that when I judge others, I am living
outside of Your will for my life. You have forgiven me,
Lord. Let me forgive others, let me love them, and let me
help them . . . without judging them. Amen

for guys

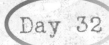

You'd Better Beware

Your love must be real. Hate what is evil,
and hold on to what is good.

ROMANS 12:9 NCV

ace facts: you live a temptation-filled world. The devil is hard at work in your neighborhood, and so are his helpers. Here in the 21st-century, the bad guys are working around the clock to lead you astray. That's why you must remain vigilant.

In a letter to believers, Peter offers a stern warning: "Your adversary, the devil, prowls around like a roaring lion, seeking someone to devour" (I Peter 5:8 NASB). What was true in New Testament times is equally true in our own. Satan tempts his prey and then devours them (and it's up to you—and only you—to make sure that you're not one of the ones being devoured!).

As a believer who seeks a radical relationship with Jesus, you must beware because temptations are everywhere. Satan is determined to win; you must be equally determined that he does not.

more stuff to think about

Christianity isn't a religion about going to Sunday school,
potluck suppers, being nice, holding car washes,
sending your secondhand clothes off to Mexico—
as good as those things might be. This is a world at war.

JOHN ELDREDGE

Of two evils, choose neither.

C. H. SPURGEON

Today's Prayer

Lord, strengthen my walk with You. Evil comes in
many disguises, and sometimes it is only with Your
help that I can recognize right from wrong. Your
presence in my life enables me to choose truth and to
live a life pleasing to You. May I always live in Your
presence. Amen

for guys

His Joy and Yours

O clap your hands, all peoples;
Shout to God with the voice of joy.

PSALM 47:1 NASB

Have you made the choice to rejoice? Hopefully so. After all, if you're a believer, you have plenty of reasons to be joyful. Yet sometimes, amid the inevitable hustle and bustle of life-here-on-earth, you may lose sight of your blessings as you wrestle with the challenges of everyday life.

Christ made it clear to His followers: He intended that His joy would become their joy. And it still holds true today: Christ intends that His believers share His love with His joy in their hearts.

What does life have in store for you? A world full of possibilities (of course, it's up to you to seize them), and God's promise of abundance (of course, it's up to you to accept it). So, as you embark upon the next phase of your journey, remember to celebrate the life that God has given you. Your Creator has blessed you beyond measure. Honor Him with your prayers, your words, your deeds, and your joy.

more stuff to think about

Joy is the serious business of heaven.

C. S. Lewis

Christ and joy go together.

E. Stanley Jones

Today's Prayer

Dear Lord, You have given me so many blessings; let me celebrate Your gifts. Make me thankful, loving, responsible, and wise. I praise You, Father, for the gift of Your Son and for the priceless gift of salvation. Make me be a joyful Christian and a worthy example to my loved ones, today and every day. Amen

for guys

Imitating Christ

Watch what God does, and then you do it, like children who learn proper behavior from their parents. Mostly what God does is love you. Keep company with him and learn a life of love. Observe how Christ loved us. His love was not cautious but extravagant. He didn't love in order to get something from us but to give everything of himself to us. Love like that.

EPHESIANS 5:1-2 MSG

Imitating Christ is impossible, but attempting to imitate Him is both possible and advisable. By attempting to imitate Jesus, we seek, to the best of our abilities, to walk in His footsteps. To the extent we succeed in following Him, we receive the spiritual abundance that is the rightful possession of those who love Christ and keep His commandments.

Do you seek God's blessings for the day ahead? Then, to the best of your abilities, imitate His Son. You will fall short, of course. But if your heart is right and your intentions are pure, God will bless your efforts, your day, and your life.

more stuff to think about

A person who gazes and keeps on gazing at Jesus
becomes like him in appearance.

E. STANLEY JONES

Christlikeness is not produced by imitation, but by
inhabitation.

RICK WARREN

Today's Prayer

Dear Jesus, because I am Your disciple, I will trust
You, I will obey Your teachings, and I will share Your
Good News. You have given me life abundant and life
eternal, and I will follow You today and forever. Amen

for guys

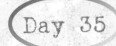
The Wisdom to be Generous

The good person is generous and lends lavishly....
PSALM 112:5 MSG

God's gifts are beyond description, His blessings beyond comprehension. God has been incredibly generous with us, and He rightfully expects us to be generous with others. That's why the thread of generosity is woven into the very fabric of God's teachings.

In the Old Testament, we are told that, "The good person is generous and lends lavishly...." (Psalm 112:5 MSG). And in the New Testament we are instructed, "Freely you have received, freely give" (Matthew 10:8 NKJV). These principles still apply. As we establish priorities for our days and our lives, we are advised to give freely of our time, our possessions, and our love—just as God has given freely to us.

Of course, we can never fully repay God for His gifts, but we can share them with others. And we should.

more stuff to think about

We are never more like God than when we give.

CHARLES SWINDOLL

Nothing is really ours until we share it.

C. S. LEWIS

Today's Prayer

Lord, You have been so generous with me; let me be generous with others. Help me to give generously of my time and my possessions as I care for those in need. And, make me a humble giver, Lord, so that all the glory and the praise might be Yours. Amen

for guys

Beyond Guilt

*There is therefore now no condemnation to those who are in
Christ Jesus, who do not walk according to the flesh,
but according to the Spirit.*

Romans 8:1 NKJV

All of us have made mistakes. Sometimes our failures
result from our own shortsightedness. On other
occasions, we are swept up in events that are beyond
our abilities to control. Under either set of circumstances,
we may experience intense feelings of guilt. But God has an
answer for the guilt that we feel. That answer, of course, is
His forgiveness.

When we ask our Heavenly Father for His forgiveness,
He forgives us completely and without reservation. Then,
we must do the difficult work of forgiving ourselves in
the same way that God has forgiven us: thoroughly and
unconditionally.

If you're feeling guilty, then it's time for a special kind
of housecleaning—a housecleaning of your mind and your
heart . . . beginning NOW!

more stuff to think about

Prayer is essential when a believer is stuck
in the pits of unresolved guilt.

CHARLES STANLEY

Guilt is a gift that leads us to grace.

FRANKLIN GRAHAM

Today's Prayer

Dear Lord, thank You for the guilt that I feel when I disobey You. Help me confess my wrongdoings, help me accept Your forgiveness, and help me renew my passion to serve You. Amen

Too Impulsive?

He who guards his lips guards his life,
but he who speaks rashly will come to ruin.
PROVERBS 13:3 NIV

A re you, at times, just a little bit impulsive? Do you occasionally leap before you look? Do you react first and think about your reaction second? If so, God wants to have a little chat with you.

God's Word is clear: as believers, we are called to lead lives of discipline, diligence, moderation, and maturity. But the world often tempts us to behave otherwise. Everywhere we turn, or so it seems, we are faced with powerful temptations to behave in undisciplined, ungodly ways.

God's Word instructs us to be disciplined in our thoughts and our actions; God's Word warns us against the dangers of impulsive behavior. God's Word teaches us that "anger" is only one letter away from "danger." And, as believers in a just God who means what He says, we should act—and react—accordingly.

more stuff to think about

Our challenge is to wait in faith for the day of God's favor and salvation.

JIM CYMBALA

Grass that is here today and gone tomorrow does not require much time to mature. A big oak tree that lasts for generations requires much more time to grow and mature. God is concerned about your life through eternity. Allow Him to take all the time He needs to shape you for His purposes. Larger assignments will require longer periods of preparation.

HENRY BLACKABY

Today's Prayer

Lord, sometimes I can be an impulsive person. Slow me down, calm me down, and help me make wise decisions . . . today and every day of my life. Amen

for guys

Extreme Faith

Whoever serves me must follow me.
Then my servant will be with me everywhere I am.
My Father will honor anyone who serves me.

JOHN 12:26 NCV

Jesus made an extreme sacrifice for you. Are you willing to make extreme changes in your life for Him? Can you honestly say that you're passionate about your faith and that you're really following Jesus? Hopefully so. But if you're preoccupied with other things—or if you're strictly a one-day-a-week Christian—then you're in need of an extreme spiritual makeover!

Jesus doesn't want you to be a run-of-the-mill, follow-the-crowd kind of guy. Jesus wants you to be a "new creation" through Him. And that's exactly what you should want for yourself, too. Nothing is more important than your wholehearted commitment to your Creator and to His only begotten Son. Your faith must never be an afterthought; it must be your ultimate priority, your ultimate possession, and your ultimate passion.

You are the recipient of Christ's love. Accept it enthusiastically and share it passionately. Jesus deserves your extreme enthusiasm; the world deserves it; and you deserve the experience of sharing it.

more stuff to think about

The essence of the Christian life is Jesus: that in all things
He might have the preeminence, not that in some things
He might have a place.

FRANKLIN GRAHAM

The heaviest end of the cross lies ever on His shoulders.
If He bids us carry a burden, He carries it also.

C. H. SPURGEON

Today's Prayer

Dear Jesus, because I am Your disciple, I will trust
You, I will obey Your teachings, and I will share Your
Good News. You have given me life abundant and life
eternal, and I will follow You today and forever. Amen

for guys

Real Joy

I've told you these things for a purpose:
that my joy might be your joy, and your joy wholly mature.
JOHN 15:11 MSG

Christ made it clear: He intends that His joy should become our joy. Yet sometimes, amid the inevitable hustle and bustle of life-here-on-earth, we can forfeit—albeit temporarily—the joy of Christ as we wrestle with the challenges of daily living.

You can't really get to know God until you genuinely experience God's joy for yourself. It's not enough to hear somebody else talk about being a joyful Christian—you must experience Christ's joy in order to understand it. Does that mean that you'll be a joy-filled believer 24 hours a day, seven days a week, from this moment on? Nope. But it does mean that you can experience God's joy personally, frequently, intensely.

So here's a prescription for better spiritual health: Open the door of your soul to Christ. When you do, He will give you peace and joy . . . heaping helpings of peace and joy.

more stuff to think about

When I met Christ, I felt that I had swallowed sunshine.

E. STANLEY JONES

Joy comes from knowing God loves me
and knows who I am and where I'm going . . .
that my future is secure as I rest in Him.

JAMES DOBSON

Today's Prayer

Dear Lord, You have given me so many blessings; let
me celebrate Your gifts. Make me thankful, loving,
responsible, and wise. I praise You, Father, for the gift of
Your Son and for the priceless gift of salvation. Make
me be a joyful Christian and a worthy example to my
loved ones, today and every day. Amen

for guys

The Marathon

*Patient endurance is what you need now,
so you will continue to do God's will.
Then you will receive all that he has promised.*

HEBREWS 10:36 NLT

Are you one of those guys who doesn't give up easily, or are you quick to bail out when the going gets tough? If you've developed the unfortunate habit of giving up at the first sign of trouble, it's probably time for you to have a heart-to-heart talk with the guy you see every time you look in the mirror.

A well-lived life is like a marathon, not a sprint—it calls for preparation, determination, and lots of perseverance. As an example of perfect perseverance, you need look no further than your Savior, Jesus Christ.

Jesus finished what He began. Despite His suffering, despite the shame of the cross, Jesus was steadfast in His faithfulness to God. You, too, should remain faithful, especially when times are tough.

Are you facing a difficult situation? If so, remember this: whatever your problem, God can handle it. Your job is to keep persevering until He does.

more stuff to think about

Battles are won in the trenches, in the grit
and grime of courageous determination;
they are won day by day in the arena of life.

CHARLES SWINDOLL

Jesus taught that perseverance is
the essential element in prayer.

E. M. BOUNDS

Today's Prayer

Lord, when life is difficult, I am tempted to abandon hope in the future. But You are my God, and I can draw strength from You. Let me trust You, Father, in good times and in bad times. Let me persevere—even if my soul is troubled—and let me follow Your Son Jesus Christ this day and forever. Amen

for guys

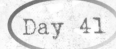

Beyond Anger

Now you must rid yourselves of all such things as these:
anger, rage, malice....
COLOSSIANS 3:8 NIV

The frustrations of everyday living can sometimes get the better of us, and we allow minor disappointments to cause us major problems. When we allow ourselves to become overly irritated by the inevitable ups and downs of life, we become overstressed, overheated, over-anxious, and just plain angry.

When you allow yourself to become angry, you are certain to defeat at least one person: yourself. When you allow the minor frustrations of everyday life to hijack your emotions, you do harm to yourself and to your loved ones. So today and every day, guard yourself against the kind of angry thinking that inevitably takes a toll on your emotions and your relationships.

As the old saying goes, "Anger usually improves nothing but the arch of a cat's back." So don't allow feelings of anger or frustration to rule your life, or, for that matter, your day—your life is simply to short for that, and you deserve much better treatment than that . . . from yourself.

more stuff to think about

When you strike out in anger, you may miss
the other person, but you will always hit yourself.

JIM GALLERY

Is there somebody who's always getting your goat?
Talk to the Shepherd.

ANONYMOUS

Today's Prayer

Lord, sometimes, I am quick to anger and slow to
forgive. But I know, Lord, that You seek abundance
and peace for my life. Forgiveness is Your
commandment; empower me to follow the example of
Your Son Jesus who forgave His persecutors. As I turn
away from anger, I claim the peace that You intend for
my life. Amen

for guys

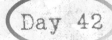

Too Busy to Pray?

*If my people who are called by my name, will humble
themselves and pray and seek my face and turn from their
wicked ways, then will I hear from heaven
and will forgive their sin and will heal their land.*

2 CHRONICLES 7:14 NIV

Is prayer an integral part of your daily life or is it a hit-
or-miss habit? Do you "pray without ceasing," or is your
prayer life an afterthought? Do you regularly pray in the
quiet moments of the early morning, or do you bow your
head only when others are watching? If your prayers have
become more a matter of habit than a matter of passion,
you're robbing yourself of a deeper relationship with God.
And how can you rectify this situation? By praying more
frequently and more fervently.

The quality of your spiritual life will be in direct
proportion to the quality of your prayer life: the more you
pray, the closer you will feel to God. So today, instead of
turning things over in your mind, turn them over to God in
prayer. Don't limit your prayers to the dinner table or the
bedside table. Pray constantly about things great and small.
God is always listening . . . and the rest is up to you.

more stuff to think about

God shapes the world by prayer. The more praying
there is in the world, the better the world will be,
and the mightier will be the forces against evil.

E. M. BOUNDS

Prayer connects us with God's limitless potential.

HENRY BLACKABY

Today's Prayer

Dear Lord, I will open my heart to You. I will take my
concerns, my fears, my plans, and my hopes to You in
prayer. And then, I will trust the answers that You give.
You are my loving Father, and I will accept Your will
for my life today and every day that I live. Amen

for guys

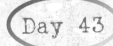

God Can Handle It

*Give your burdens to the Lord, and he will take care of you.
He will not permit the godly to slip and fall.*

PSALM 55:22 NLT

It's a promise that is made over and over again in the
Bible: Whatever "it" is, God can handle it.

Life isn't always easy. Far from it! Sometimes, life can be
very, very tough. But even then, even during our darkest
moments, we're protected by a loving Heavenly Father.
When we're worried, God can reassure us; when we're sad,
God can comfort us. When our hearts are broken, God is
not just near, He is here. So we must lift our thoughts and
prayers to Him. When we do, He will answer our prayers.
Why? Because He is our shepherd, and He has promised to
protect us now and forever.

more stuff to think about

You may not know what you are going to do;
you only know that God knows what He is going to do.

OSWALD CHAMBERS

The next time you're disappointed, don't panic.
Don't give up. Just be patient and let God remind you
He's still in control.

MAX LUCADO

Today's Prayer

Dear Lord, You rule over our world, and I will allow You
to rule over my heart. I will obey Your commandments,
I will study Your Word, and I will seek Your will for
my life, today and every day of my life. Amen

for guys

Who Rules?

First pay attention to me, and then relax.
Now you can take it easy—you're in good hands.
PROVERBS 1:33 MSG

Is God a big priority for you . . . or is He an afterthought? Do you give God your best or what's left? Have you given Christ your heart, your soul, your talents, your time, and your testimony? Or are you giving Him little more than a few hours each Sunday morning?

In the book of Exodus, God warns that we should place no gods before Him (Exodus 20:3). Yet all too often, we place our Lord in second, third, or fourth place as we worship the gods of pride, money, or personal gratification. When we unwittingly place possessions or relationships above our love for the Creator, we must realign our priorities or suffer the consequences.

Does God rule your heart? Make certain that the honest answer to this question is a resounding yes. In the life of every radical believer, God comes first. And that's precisely the place that He deserves in your heart.

more stuff to think about

He is no fool who gives what he cannot keep
to gain what he cannot lose.

JIM ELLIOT

Having values keeps a person focused on
the important things.

JOHN MAXWELL

Today's Prayer

Dear Lord, today is a new day. Help me finish
the important tasks first, even if those tasks are
unpleasant. Don't let me put off until tomorrow what I
should do today. Amen

for guys

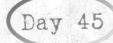

When Mountains Need Moving

I tell you the truth, you can say to this mountain,
"Go, fall into the sea." And if you have no doubts
in your mind and believe that what you say will happen,
God will do it for you.

MARK 11:23 NCV

Because we live in a demanding world, all of us have mountains to climb and mountains to move. Moving those mountains requires faith.

Every life—including yours—is a series of wins and losses. Every step of the way, through every triumph and tragedy, God walks with you, ready and willing to strengthen you. So the next time you find your courage tested to the limit, remember to take your fears to God. If you call upon Him, you will be comforted. Whatever your challenge, whatever your trouble, God can handle it.

When you place your faith, your trust, indeed your life in the hands of your Heavenly Father, you'll be amazed at the marvelous things He can do with you and through you. So strengthen your faith through praise, through worship, through Bible study, and through prayer. And trust God's plans. With Him, all things are possible, and He stands ready to open a world of possibilities to you . . . if you have faith.

more stuff to think about

Only God can move mountains,
but faith and prayer can move God.

E. M. BOUNDS

I do not want merely to possess a faith;
I want a faith that possesses me.

CHARLES KINGSLEY

Today's Prayer

Dear Lord, I want faith that moves mountains. You have big plans for this world and big plans for me. Help me fulfill those plans, Father, as I follow in the footsteps of Your Son. Amen

for guys

The Search for Purpose

For everything, absolutely everything, above and below, visible and invisible, rank after rank after rank of angels— everything got started in him and finds its purpose in him.

COLOSSIANS 1:16 MSG

"What on earth does God intend for me to do with my life?" It's an easy question to ask but, for many of us, a difficult question to answer. Why? Because God's purposes aren't always clear to us. Sometimes we wander aimlessly in a wilderness of our own making. And sometimes, we struggle mightily against God in an unsuccessful attempt to find success and happiness through our own means, not His.

Are you genuinely trying to figure out God's purpose for your life? If so, you can be sure that with God's help, you will eventually discover it. So keep praying, and keep watching. And rest assured: God's got big plans for you . . . very big plans.

more stuff to think about

Oh Lord, let me not live to be useless.

JOHN WESLEY

When God speaks to you through the Bible, prayer, circumstances, the church, or in some other way, he has a purpose in mind for your life.

HENRY BLACKABY AND CLAUDE KING

Today's Prayer

Dear Lord, let Your purposes be my purposes. Let Your priorities be my priorities. Let Your will be my will. Let Your Word be my guide. And, let me grow in faith and in wisdom today and every day. Amen

for guys

Need Strength?

Create in me a pure heart, O God, and renew a steadfast spirit within me. Do not cast me from your presence or take your Holy Spirit from me. Restore to me the joy of your salvation and grant me a willing spirit, to sustain me.

PSALM 51:10-12 NIV

Even the most inspired Christian guys can find themselves running on empty. Even the most well intentioned guys can run out of energy; even the most hopeful believers can be burdened by fears and doubts. And you are no exception.

God intends that His children lead joyous lives filled with abundance and peace. But sometimes, abundance and peace seem very far away. During these difficult days, we must turn to God for renewal, and when we do, He will restore us.

Are you tired or troubled? Turn your heart toward God in prayer. Are you weak or worried? Take the time—or, more accurately, make the time—to delve deeply into God's Holy Word. Are you spiritually depleted? Call upon fellow believers to support you, and call upon Christ to renew your spirit and your life. When you do, you'll discover that the Creator of the universe stands always ready and always able to create a new sense of wonderment and joy in you.

more stuff to think about

The resurrection of Jesus Christ is the power of God
to change history and to change lives.

BILL BRIGHT

Walking with God leads to receiving his intimate counsel,
and counseling leads to deep restoration.

JOHN ELDREDGE

Today's Prayer

Dear Lord, sometimes the demands of the day leave
me discouraged and frustrated. Renew my strength,
Father, and give me patience and perspective. Today
and every day, let me draw comfort and courage from
Your promises, from Your love, and from Your Son.
Amen

for guys

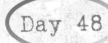

Forgiveness Now

Then Peter came to him and asked, "Lord, how often should I
forgive someone who sins against me? Seven times?"
"No!" Jesus replied, "seventy times seven!"
MATTHEW 18:21-22 NLT

Are you the kind of guy who carries a grudge? If
so, you know sometimes it's very tough to forgive
the people who have hurt you. And that's too
bad because life would be much simpler if we could
forgive people "once and for all" and be done with it. But
forgiveness is seldom that easy. For most of us, the decision
to forgive is straightforward, but the process of forgiving is
more difficult. Forgiveness is a journey that requires effort,
time, perseverance, and prayer.

Forgiveness is seldom easy, but it is always right. When
we forgive those who have hurt us, we honor God by
obeying His commandments. But when we harbor bitterness
against others, we disobey God—with predictably unhappy
results.

If you sincerely wish to forgive someone, pray for that
person. And then pray for yourself by asking God to heal
your heart. Don't expect forgiveness to be easy or quick, but
rest assured: with God as your partner, you can forgive . . .
and you will.

more stuff to think about

Learning how to forgive and forget is one of
the secrets of a happy Christian life.

WARREN WIERSBE

There is always room for more loving forgiveness
within our homes.

JAMES DOBSON

Today's Prayer

Heavenly Father, forgiveness is Your commandment,
and I know that I should forgive others just as You have
forgiven me. But, genuine forgiveness is difficult. Help
me to forgive those who have injured me, and deliver me
from the traps of anger and bitterness. Forgiveness is
Your way, Lord; let it be mine. Amen

for guys

Enthused About Life

Whatever you do, work at it with all your heart,
as working for the Lord, not for men.

COLOSSIANS 3:23 NIV

D o you see each day as a glorious opportunity to serve God and to do His will? Are you enthused about life, or do you struggle through each day giving scarcely a thought to God's blessings? Are you constantly praising God for His gifts, and are you sharing His Good News with the world? Are you excited about the possibilities for service that God has placed before you, whether at home, at work, at church, or at school? You should be.

You are the recipient of Christ's sacrificial love. Accept it enthusiastically, and share it fervently. Jesus deserves your enthusiasm; the world deserves it; and you deserve the experience of sharing it.

more stuff to think about

Catch on fire with enthusiasm and people will come
for miles to watch you burn.

JOHN WESLEY

Wherever you are, be all there. Live to the hilt
every situation you believe to be the will of God.

JIM ELLIOT

Today's Prayer

Dear Lord, You have called me not to a life of
mediocrity, but to a life of passion. Today, I will be an
enthusiastic follower of Your Son, and I will share His
Good News—and His love—with all who cross my path.
Amen

for guys

Excuses Everywhere

People's own foolishness ruins their lives,
but in their minds they blame the Lord.
PROVERBS 19:3 NCV

Excuses are everywhere . . . excellence is not. Whether you're a student or a corporate CEO, your work is a picture book of your priorities. So whatever your job description, it's up to you, and no one else, to become masterful at your craft. It's up to you to do your job right, and to do it right now.

Because we humans are such creative excuse-makers, all of the best excuses have already been taken—we've heard them all before.

So if you're wasting your time trying to concoct a new and improved excuse, don't bother. It's impossible. A far better strategy is this: do the work. Now. Then, let your excellent work speak loudly and convincingly for itself.

more stuff to think about

Replace your excuses with fresh determination.

CHARLES SWINDOLL

An excuse is only the skin of a reason stuffed with a lie.

VANCE HAVNER

Today's Prayer

Dear Lord, when I make a mistake, I want to admit it. Help me not blame others for the mistakes that I make. And when I make a mistake, help me to learn from it. Amen

for guys

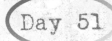
Using Your Gifts

This is why I remind you to keep using the gift God
gave you when I laid my hands on you. Now let it grow,
as a small flame grows into a fire.

2 TIMOTHY 1:6 NCV

F ace it: you've got an array of talents that need to be
refined. All people possess special gifts—bestowed
from the Father above—and you are no exception.
But, your gift is no guarantee of success; it must be
cultivated—by you—or it will go unused . . . and God's gift
to you will be squandered.

Today, make a promise to yourself that you will earnestly
seek to discover the talents that God has given you. Then,
nourish those talents and make them grow. Finally, vow to
share your gifts with the world for as long as God gives you
the power to do so. After all, the best way to say "Thank
You" for God's gifts is to use them.

more stuff to think about

You are the only person on earth who can use your ability.

ZIG ZIGLAR

God often reveals His direction for our lives through
the way He made us…with a certain personality
and unique skills.

BILL HYBELS

Today's Prayer

Lord, I praise You for Your priceless gifts. I give thanks
for Your creation, for Your Son, and for the unique
talents and opportunities that You have given me. Let
me use my gifts for the glory of Your kingdom, this
day and every day. Amen

for guys

Too Many Distractions?

Look straight ahead, and fix your eyes on what lies before you. Mark out a straight path for your feet; then stick to the path and stay safe. Don't get sidetracked; keep your feet from following evil.

PROVERBS 4:25-27 NLT

All of us must live through those days when the traffic jams, the computer crashes, and the dog makes a main course out of our homework. But, when we find ourselves distracted by the minor frustrations of life, we must catch ourselves, take a deep breath, and lift our thoughts upward.

Although we may, at times, struggle mightily to rise above the distractions of everyday living, we need never struggle alone. God is here—eternal and faithful, with infinite patience and love—and, if we reach out to Him, He will restore our sense of perspective and give peace to our souls.

more stuff to think about

Paul did one thing. Most of us dabble in forty things.
Are you a doer or a dabbler?

VANCE HAVNER

As long as Jesus is one of many options, He is no option.

MAX LUCADO

Today's Prayer

Dear Lord, help me to face this day with a spirit of
optimism and thanksgiving. And let me focus my
thoughts on You and Your incomparable gifts. Amen

for guys

You and Your Conscience

If the way you live isn't consistent with what you believe,
then it's wrong.
ROMANS 14:23 MSG

Billy Graham correctly observed, "Most of us follow our conscience as we follow a wheelbarrow. We push it in front of us in the direction we want to go." To do so, of course, is a profound mistake. Yet all of us, on occasion, have failed to listen to the voice that God planted in our hearts, and all of us have suffered the consequences.

God gave you a conscience for a very good reason: to make your path conform to His will. Wise believers make it a practice to listen carefully to that quiet internal voice. Count yourself among that number. When your conscience speaks, listen and learn. In all likelihood, God is trying to get His message through. And in all likelihood, it is a message that you desperately need to hear.

more stuff to think about

The beginning of backsliding means your conscience
does not answer to the truth.

OSWALD SANDERS

The convicting work of the Holy Spirit awakens,
disturbs, and judges.

FRANKLIN GRAHAM

Today's Prayer

Dear Lord, You speak to me through the gift of Your
Holy Word. And, Father, You speak to me through that
still small voice that tells me right from wrong. Let me
follow Your way, Lord, and, in these quiet moments,
show me Your plan for this day, that I might serve You.
Amen

for guys

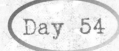

God Is Love

Unfailing love surrounds those who trust the LORD.
PSALM 32:10 NLT

The Bible makes this promise: God is love. It's a sweeping statement, a profoundly important description of what God is and how God works. God's love is perfect. When we open our hearts to His perfect love, we are touched by the Creator's hand, and we are transformed.

Today, even if you can only carve out a few quiet moments, offer sincere prayers of thanksgiving to your Creator. He loves you now and throughout all eternity. Open your heart to His presence and His love.

more stuff to think about

The life of faith is a daily exploration of
the constant and countless ways in which God's grace
and love are experienced.

EUGENE PETERSON

If you have an obedience problem, you have a love
problem. Focus your attention on God's love.

HENRY BLACKABY

Today's Prayer

Thank You, Dear God, for Your love. You are my loving
Father. I thank You for Your love and for Your Son. I
will praise You; I will worship You; and, I will love You
today, tomorrow, and forever. Amen

for guys

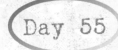

Beyond Fear

I sought the Lord, and He answered me
and delivered me from all my fears.
PSALM 34:4 HCSB

We live in a world that is, at times, a frightening place. We live in a world that is, at times, a discouraging place. We live in a world where life-changing losses can be so painful and so profound that it seems we will never recover. But, with God's help, and with the help of encouraging family members and friends, we can recover.

During the darker days of life, we are wise to remember the words of Jesus, who reassured His disciples, saying, "Take courage! It is I. Don't be afraid" (Matthew 14:27 NIV). Then, with God's comfort and His love in our hearts, we can offer encouragement to others. And by helping them face their fears, we can, in turn, tackle our own problems with courage, determination, and faith.

more stuff to think about

The Lord Jesus by His Holy Spirit is with me,
and the knowledge of His presence dispels the darkness
and allays any fears.

BILL BRIGHT

When we meditate on God and remember
the promises He has given us in His Word,
our faith grows, and our fears dissolve.

CHARLES STANLEY

Today's Prayer

Your Word reminds me, Lord, that even when I walk through the valley of the shadow of death, I need fear no evil, for You are with me, and You comfort me. Thank You, Lord, for a perfect love that casts out fear. Let me live courageously and faithfully this day and every day. Amen

for guys

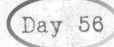

Discipline Now

But I discipline my body and bring it into subjection,
lest, when I have preached to others,
I myself should become disqualified.

1 Corinthians 9:27 NKJV

God doesn't reward laziness, misbehavior, or apathy. To the contrary, He expects His followers to behave with dignity and discipline. But sometimes, it's extremely difficult to be dignified and disciplined. Why? Because the world wants us to believe that dignified, self-disciplined behavior is going out of style.

Face facts: Life's greatest rewards aren't likely to fall into your lap. To the contrary, your greatest accomplishments will probably require lots of work, which is perfectly fine with God. After all, He knows that you're up to the task, and He has big plans for you. God will do His part to fulfill those plans, and the rest, of course, is up to you.

Now, are you steadfast in your determination to be a self-disciplined guy? If so, congratulations . . . if not, reread this little essay—and keep reading it—until God's message finally sinks in.

more stuff to think about

The alternative to discipline is disaster.

VANCE HAVNER

Personal humility is a spiritual discipline
and the hallmark of the service of Jesus.

FRANKLIN GRAHAM

Today's Prayer

Heavenly Father, make me a man of discipline and
righteousness. Let me teach others by the faithfulness
of my conduct, and let me follow Your will and Your
Word, today and every day. Amen

for guys

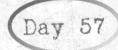

Good Decision

God's Way is not a matter of mere talk;
it's an empowered life.

1 CORINTHIANS 4:20 MSG

Everyday life is an adventure in decision-making. Each day, we make countless decisions that hopefully bring us closer to God. When we obey God's commandments, we share in His abundance and His peace. But, when we turn our backs upon God by disobeying Him, we invite Old Man Trouble to stop by for an extended visit.

Do you want to be successful and happy? If so, here's a good place to start: Obey God. When you're faced with a difficult choice or a powerful temptation, pray about it. Invite God into your heart and live according to His commandments. When you do, you will be blessed today, and tomorrow, and forever.

more stuff to think about

If we don't hunger and thirst after righteousness,
we'll become anemic and feel miserable
in our Christian experience.

FRANKLIN GRAHAM

Righteousness not only defines God,
but God defines righteousness.

BILL HYBELS

Today's Prayer

Lord, it is so much easier to speak of the righteous life
than it is to live it. Let me live righteously, and let my
actions be consistent with my beliefs. Let every step
that I take reflect Your truth, and let me live a life that
is worthy of Your Son. Amen

for guys

Gimme Patience!

Be gentle to everyone, able to teach, and patient.
2 TIMOTHY 2:23 HCSB

Are you a perfectly patient fellow? If so, feel free to skip the rest of this page. But if you're not, here's something to think about: If you really want to become a more patient person, God is ready and willing to help.

The Bible promises that when you sincerely seek God's help, He will give you the things that you need—and that includes patience. But God won't force you to become a more patient person. If you want to become a more mature Christian, you've got to do some of the work yourself—and the best time to start doing that work is now.

So, if you want to gain patience and maturity, bow your head and start praying about it. Then, rest assured that with God's help, you can most certainly make yourself a more patient, understanding, mature Christian.

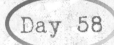

more stuff to think about

As we wait on God, He helps us use the winds of
adversity to soar above our problems.
As the Bible says, "Those who wait on the LORD . . .
shall mount up with wings like eagles."

BILLY GRAHAM

You can't step in front of God and not get in trouble.
When He says, "Go three steps," don't go four.

CHARLES STANLEY

Today's Prayer

Heavenly Father, let me wait quietly for You. Let me
live according to Your plan and according to Your
timetable. When I am hurried, slow me down. When I
become impatient with others, give me empathy. Today,
I want to be a patient Christian, Dear Lord, as I trust in
You and in Your master plan. Amen

for guys

A Willingness to Serve

You address me as 'Teacher' and 'Master,' and rightly so.
That is what I am. So if I, the Master and Teacher,
washed your feet, you must now wash each other's feet.
I've laid down a pattern for you. What I've done, you do.
JOHN 13:15 MSG

The words of Jesus are clear: the most esteemed men and women in this world are not the big-shots who jump up on stage and hog the spotlight; the greatest among us are those who are willing to become humble servants.

Today, you may be tempted to take more than you give. But if you feel the urge to be selfish, resist that urge with all your might. Don't be stingy, selfish, or self-absorbed. Instead, serve your friends quietly and without fanfare. Find a need and fill it . . . humbly. Lend a helping hand…anonymously. Share a word of kindness . . . with quiet sincerity. As you go about your daily activities, remember that the Savior of all humanity made Himself a servant, and we, as His followers, must do no less.

more stuff to think about

God does not do anything with us, only through us.

OSWALD CHAMBERS

In Jesus, the service of God and the service
of the least of the brethren were one.

DIETRICH BONHOEFFER

Today's Prayer

Dear Lord, when Jesus humbled Himself and became a
servant, He also became an example for me. Make me a
faithful steward of my gifts, and let me be a humble
servant to my loved ones, to my friends, and to those
in need. Amen

for guys

Choices

*I am offering you life or death, blessings or curses.
Now, choose life! . . . To choose life is to love
the Lord your God, obey him, and stay close to him.*

DEUTERONOMY 30:19-20 NCV

As a believer who has been transformed by the radical love of Jesus, you have every reason to make wise choices. But sometimes, when the daily grind threatens to grind you up and spit you out, you may make choices that are displeasing to God. When you do, you'll pay a price because you'll forfeit the happiness and the peace that might otherwise have been yours.

So, as you pause to consider the kind of Christian you are—and the kind of Christian you want to become—ask yourself whether you're sitting on the fence or standing in the light. And then, if you sincerely want to follow in the footsteps of the One from Galilee, make choices that are pleasing to Him. He deserves no less . . . and neither, for that matter, do you.

more stuff to think about

Every day, I find countless opportunities to decide
whether I will obey God and demonstrate my love for Him
or try to please myself or the world system.
God is waiting for my choices.

BILL BRIGHT

Life is a series of choices between the bad, the good,
and the best. Everything depends on how we choose.

VANCE HAVNER

Today's Prayer

Heavenly Father, I have many choices to make. Help me
choose wisely as I follow in the footsteps of Your only
begotten Son. Amen

for guys

Fully Grown?

So let us stop going over the basics of Christianity again and again. Let us go on instead and become mature in our understanding.

HEBREWS 6:1 NLT

A re you about as mature as you're ever going to be? Hopefully not! When it comes to your faith, God doesn't intend for you to become "fully grown," at least not in this lifetime.

As a Christian, you should continue to grow in the love and the knowledge of your Savior as long as you live. How? By studying God's Word, by obeying His commandments, and by allowing His Son to reign over your heart.

Are you continually seeking to become a more mature believer? Hopefully so, because that's exactly what you owe to God and to yourself.

more stuff to think about

A person who gazes and keeps on gazing at Jesus
becomes like him in appearance.

E. STANLEY JONES

The Scriptures were not given for our information,
but for our transformation.

D. L. MOODY

Today's Prayer

Dear Lord, the Bible tells me that You are at work in my
life, continuing to help me grow and to mature in my
faith. Show me Your wisdom, Father, and let me live
according to Your Word and Your will. Amen

for guys

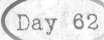
Saying "Thanks" to God

Give thanks in all circumstances;
for this is God's will for you in Christ Jesus.

1 THESSALONIANS 5:18 NIV

Are you basically a thankful guy? Do you appreciate the stuff you've got and the life that you're privileged to live? You most certainly should be thankful. After all, when you stop to think about it, God has given you more blessings than you can count. So the question of the day is this: will you slow down long enough to thank your Heavenly Father . . . or not?

Sometimes, life-here-on-earth can be complicated, demanding, and frustrating. When the demands of life leave you rushing from place to place with scarcely a moment to spare, you may fail to pause and thank your Creator for the countless blessings He has given you. Failing to thank God is understandable . . . but it's wrong.

God's Word makes it clear: a wise heart is a thankful heart. Period. Your Heavenly Father has blessed you beyond measure, and you owe Him everything, including your thanks. God is always listening—are you willing to say thanks? It's up to you, and the next move is yours.

2 minutes A DAY

more stuff to think about

It is only with gratitude that life becomes rich.

DIETRICH BONHOEFFER

We ought to give thanks for all fortune: if it is good,
because it is good, if bad, because it works in us patience,
humility, and the contempt of this world along with
the hope of our eternal country.

C. S. LEWIS

Today's Prayer

Dear Lord, today I will thank You for all Your
blessings. And I'll do the same thing tomorrow, and
every day after that. You never stop loving me, and I
will never stop praising You. Amen

for guys

Getting the Work Done

Do not be lazy but work hard,
serving the Lord with all your heart.
ROMANS 12:11 NCV

God's Word teaches us the value of hard work. In his second letter to the Thessalonians, Paul warns, " ...if any would not work, neither should he eat" (3:10 KJV). And the Book of Proverbs proclaims, "One who is slack in his work is brother to one who destroys" (18:9 NIV). In short, God has created a world in which diligence is rewarded and laziness is not. So, whatever it is that you choose to do, do it with commitment, excitement, and vigor. And remember this: Hard work is not simply a proven way to get ahead, it's also part of God's plan for you.

You have countless opportunities to accomplish great things for God—but you should not expect the work to be easy. So pray as if everything depended upon God, but work as if everything depended upon you. When you do, you should expect very big payoffs because when you and God become partners in your work, amazing things happen.

more stuff to think about

If you want to reach your potential,
you need to add a strong work ethic to your talent.

JOHN MAXWELL

Chiefly the mold of a man's fortune is in his own hands.

FRANCIS BACON

Today's Prayer

Lord, let me be an industrious worker in Your fields.
Those fields are ripe, Lord, and Your workers are few.
Let me be counted as Your faithful, diligent servant
today, and every day. Amen

for guys

The Wisdom of Waiting

God wants you to live a pure life. Keep yourselves from sexual promiscuity. Learn to appreciate and give dignity to your body, not abusing it, as is so common among those who know nothing of God.

1 THESSALONIANS 4:3-5 MSG

You live in a society that is filled to the brim with temptations, distractions, and distortions about sex. You are bombarded with images that glamorize sex outside marriage. In fact, you are subjected to daily pressures and problems that were largely unknown to earlier generations. At every corner, or so it seems, you are confronted with the message that premarital sex is a harmless activity, something that should be considered "recreational." That message is a terrible lie with tragic consequences.

When you think about it, the argument in favor of abstinence isn't a very hard case to make. First and foremost, abstinence is a part of God's plan for people who are not married. Period. But it doesn't stop there: abstinence is also the right thing to do and the smart thing to do.

God has a plan for your life, a plan that does not include sex before marriage. So do yourself a favor: take time to think carefully about the wisdom of waiting. It's your choice. Please choose wisely.

more stuff to think about

To many, total abstinence is easier than perfect moderation.
ST. AUGUSTINE

To wait upon God is the perfection of activity.
OSWALD CHAMBERS

Today's Prayer

Dear Lord, Your Word makes it clear I am to honor You
by honoring my body. In every decision that I make,
I will obey my conscience and obey Your Holy Word.
Amen.

for guys

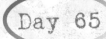

Day 65

Courage for Difficult Days

Be strong and courageous, and do the work.
Do not be afraid or discouraged, for the Lord God,
my God, is with you.

1 CHRONICLES 28:20 NIV

Life-here-on-earth can be difficult and discouraging at times. During our darkest moments, God offers us strength and courage if we turn our hearts and our prayers to Him.

As believing Christians, we have every reason to live courageously. After all, the ultimate battle has already been fought and won on the cross at Calvary. But sometimes, because we are imperfect human beings who possess imperfect faith, we fall prey to fear and doubt. The answer to our fears, of course, is God.

The next time you find your courage tested to the limit, remember that God is as near as your next breath. He is your shield and your strength; He is your protector and your deliverer. Call upon Him in your hour of need and then be comforted. Whatever your challenge, whatever your trouble, God can handle it . . . and will!

2 minutes a day

more stuff to think about

The fear of God is the death of every other fear.

C. H. SPURGEON

Do not let Satan deceive you into being afraid of God's plans for your life.

R. A. TORREY

Today's Prayer

Lord, sometimes, this world is a fearful place. Yet, You have promised me that You are with me always. With You as my protector, I am not afraid. Today, Dear Lord, I will live courageously as I place my trust in Your everlasting power and my faith in Your everlasting love. Amen

for guys

Considering the Cross

But God forbid that I should boast except in the cross of our Lord Jesus Christ, by whom the world has been crucified to me, and I to the world.

GALATIANS 6:14 NKJV

As we consider Christ's sacrifice on the cross, we should be profoundly humbled and profoundly grateful. And today, as we come to Christ in prayer, we should do so in a spirit of quiet, heartfelt devotion to the One who gave His life so that we might have life eternal.

He was the Son of God, but He wore a crown of thorns. He was the Savior of mankind, yet He was put to death on a roughhewn cross made of wood. He offered His healing touch to an unsaved world, and yet the same hands that had healed the sick and raised the dead were pierced with nails.

Christ humbled Himself on a cross—for you. He shed His blood—for you. He has offered to walk with you through this life and throughout all eternity. As you approach Him today in prayer, think about His sacrifice and His grace. And be humble.

more stuff to think about

There is no detour to holiness.
Jesus came to the resurrection through the cross,
not around it.

LEIGHTON FORD

No man understands the Scriptures
unless he is acquainted with the cross.

MARTIN LUTHER

Today's Prayer

Dear Jesus, You are my Savior and my protector. You suffered on the cross for me, and I will give You honor and praise every day of my life. I will honor you with my words, my thoughts, and my prayers. And I will live according to Your commandments, so that thorough me, others might come to know Your perfect love. Amen

for guys

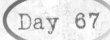
Time to Praise God

*I will praise you, Lord, with all my heart. I will tell all
the miracles you have done. I will be happy because of you;
God Most High, I will sing praises to your name.*

PSALM 9:1-2 NCV

If you're like most guys on the planet, you're a very busy
fellow. Your life is probably hectic, demanding, and
complicated. When the demands of life leave you rushing
from place to place with scarcely a moment to spare, you
may fail to pause and thank your Creator for the blessings
He has bestowed upon you. Big mistake.

No matter how busy you are, you should never be too
busy to thank God for His gifts. Your task, as an extreme
follower of the living Christ, is to praise God many times
each day. After all, your Heavenly Father has blessed you
beyond measure, and you owe Him everything, including
your thanks, starting now.

more stuff to think about

Praise opens the window of our hearts, preparing us to walk more closely with God. Prayer raises the window of our spirit, enabling us to listen more clearly to the Father.

MAX LUCADO

Be not afraid of saying too much in the praises of God; all the danger is of saying too little.

MATTHEW HENRY

Today's Prayer

Heavenly Father, I come to You today with hope in my heart and praise on my lips. Make me a faithful steward of the blessings You have entrusted to me. Let me follow in Christ's footsteps today and every day that I live. And let my words and deeds praise You now and forever. Amen

for guys

Not in Denial

For everyone who practices wicked things hates the light and avoids it, so that his deeds may not be exposed. But anyone who lives by the truth comes to the light, so that his works may be shown to be accomplished by God.

JOHN 3:20–21 HCSB

If we deny our sins, we allow those sins to flourish. And if we allow sinful behaviors to become habits, we invite hardships into our own lives and into the lives of our loved ones. When we yield to the distractions and temptations of this troubled world, we suffer. But God has other intentions, and His plans for our lives do not include sin or denial.

When we allow ourselves to encounter God's presence, He will lead us away from temptation, away from confusion, and away from the self-deception. God is the champion of truth and the enemy of denial. May we see ourselves through His eyes and conduct ourselves accordingly.

more stuff to think about

There's none so blind as those who will not see.

MATTHEW HENRY

Man prefers to believe what he prefers to be true.

FRANCIS BACON

Today's Prayer

Dear Lord, help me see the truth, and help me respond to the things that I see with determination, wisdom, and courage. Amen

for guys

Big Dreams

With God's power working in us, God can do much,
much more than anything we can ask or imagine.
EPHESIANS 3:20 NCV

Are you willing to entertain the possibility that God has big plans in store for you? Hopefully so. Yet sometimes, especially if you've recently experienced a life-altering disappointment, you may find it difficult to envision a brighter future for yourself and your family. If so, it's time to reconsider your own capabilities . . . and God's.

Your heavenly Father created you with unique gifts and untapped talents; your job is to tap them. When you do, you'll begin to feel an increasing sense of confidence in yourself and in your future.

It takes courage to dream big dreams. You will discover that courage when you do three things: accept the past, trust God to handle the future, and make the most of the time He has given you today.

Nothing is too difficult for God, and no dreams are too big for Him—not even yours. So start living—and dreaming—accordingly.

more stuff to think about

You cannot out-dream God.

JOHN ELDREDGE

To make your dream come true, you have to stay awake.

DENNIS SWANBERG

Today's Prayer

Dear Lord, give me the courage to dream and the faithfulness to trust in Your perfect plan. When I am worried or weary, give me strength for today and hope for tomorrow. Keep me mindful of Your healing power, Your infinite love, and Your eternal salvation. Amen

for guys

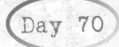

The Book He Wrote

You will be a good servant of Christ Jesus, constantly nourished on the words of the faith and of the sound doctrine which you have been following.

1 TIMOTHY 4:6 NASB

If you want to know God, you should read the book He wrote. It's called the Bible, and it is one of the most important tools that God uses to direct your steps and transform your life.

As you seek to build a deeper relationship with your Creator, you must decide whether God's Word will be bright spotlight that guides your path every day or a tiny nightlight that occasionally flickers in the dark. The decision to study the Bible—or not—is yours and yours alone. But make no mistake: the way that you choose to use your Bible will have a profound impact on you and your loved ones.

The Bible is unlike any other book. It is a priceless gift from your Creator, a tool that God intends for you to use in every aspect of your life. And, it contains promises upon which you, as a Christian, can and must depend.

God's Holy Word is, indeed, a life-changing, one-of-a-kind treasure. Handle it with care, but more importantly, handle it every day.

more stuff to think about

Reading news without reading the Bible will
inevitably lead to an unbalanced life, an anxious spirit,
a worried and depressed soul.

BILL BRIGHT

Try to get saturated with the gospel.

C. H. SPURGEON

Today's Prayer

Heavenly Father, Your Word is a light unto the world; I
will study it and trust it, and share it. In all that I do,
help me be a worthy witness for You as I share the Good
News of Your perfect Son and Your perfect Word. Amen

for guys

The Right Path

The LORD says, "I will guide you along the best pathway for your life. I will advise you and watch over you."
PSALM 32:8 NLT

What does God require of us? That we worship Him only, that we welcome His Son into our hearts, and that we walk humbly with our Creator.

When Jesus was tempted by Satan, the Master's response was unambiguous. Jesus chose to worship the Lord and serve Him only. We, as followers of Christ, must follow in His footsteps.

When we place God in a position of secondary importance, we do ourselves great harm and we put ourselves at great risk. But when we place God squarely in the center of our lives—when we walk humbly and obediently with Him—we are blessed and we are protected.

more stuff to think about

Only by walking with God can we hope to find
the path that leads to life.

JOHN ELDREDGE

To walk out of His will is to walk into nowhere.

C. S. LEWIS

Today's Prayer

Lord, sometimes life is difficult. But even when I can't
see any hope for the future, You are always with me.
And, I can live courageously because I know that You
are leading me to a place where I can accomplish Your
kingdom's work . . . and where You lead, I will follow.
Amen

for guys

The Good News

*Grace to you and peace from God our Father
and the Lord Jesus Christ.*

PHILIPPIANS 1:2 NASB

Here's the great news: God's grace is not earned . . . and thank goodness it's not! If God's grace were some sort of reward for good behavior, none of us could earn enough brownie points to win the big prize. But it doesn't work that way. Grace is a free offer from God. By accepting that offer, we transform our lives today and forever.

God's grace is not just any old gift; it's the ultimate gift, and we owe Him our eternal gratitude. Our Heavenly Father is waiting patiently for each of us to accept His Son and receive His grace. Let us accept that gift today so that we might enjoy God's presence now and throughout all eternity.

more stuff to think about

You don't earn grace, and you don't deserve grace;
you simply receive it as God's loving gift,
and then share it with others.

WARREN WIERSBE

The grace of God is sufficient for all our needs, for every
problem, and for every difficulty, for every broken heart,
and for every human sorrow.

PETER MARSHALL

Today's Prayer

Lord, You have saved me by Your grace. Keep me
mindful that Your grace is a gift that I can accept but
cannot earn. I praise You for that priceless gift, today
and forever. Let me share the good news of Your grace
with a world that desperately needs Your healing touch.
Amen

for guys

Doing the Right Thing

*Pray this way for kings and all others who are in authority,
so that we can live in peace and quietness,
in godliness and dignity.*

1 TIMOTHY 2:2 NLT

Okay pal, answer this question honestly: Do you behave differently because of your relationship with Jesus? Or do you behave in pretty much the same way that you would if you weren't a believer? Hopefully, the fact that you've invited Christ to reign over your heart means that you've made BIG changes in your thoughts and your actions.

Doing the right thing is not always easy, especially when you're tired or frustrated. But, doing the wrong thing almost always leads to trouble. And sometimes, it leads to BIG trouble.

If you're determined to follow "the crowd," you may soon find yourself headed in the wrong direction. So here's some advice: Don't follow the crowd—follow Jesus. And keep following Him every day of your life, beginning with this day.

more stuff to think about

The purity of motive determines the quality of action.

OSWALD CHAMBERS

The best evidence of our having the truth is
our walking in the truth.

MATTHEW HENRY

Today's Prayer

Lord, there is a right way and a wrong way to live. Let
me live according to Your rules, not the world's rules.
Your path is right for me, God; let me follow it every
day of my life. Amen

for guys

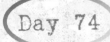
Your Bright Future

What a God we have! And how fortunate we are to have him, this Father of our Master Jesus! Because Jesus was raised from the dead, we've been given a brand-new life and have everything to live for, including a future in heaven—and the future starts now!

1 PETER 1:3-4 MSG

How bright is your future? Well, if you're a faithful believer, God's plans for you are so bright that you'd better wear shades. But here's an important question: How bright do you believe your future to be? Are you expecting a terrific tomorrow, or are you dreading a terrible one? The answer you give will have a powerful impact on the way tomorrow turns out.

Do you trust in the ultimate goodness of God's plan for your life? Will you face tomorrow's challenges with optimism and hope? You should. After all, God created you for a very important reason: His reason. And you still have important work to do: His work.

Today, as you live in the present and look to the future, remember that God has an amazing plan for you. Act—and believe—accordingly.

2 MINUTES A DAY

more stuff to think about

The Christian believes in a fabulous future.

BILLY GRAHAM

The pages of your past cannot be rewritten,
but the pages of your tomorrows are blank.

ZIG ZIGLAR

Today's Prayer

Dear Lord, as I look to the future, I will place my trust in You. If I become discouraged, I will turn to You. If I am afraid, I will seek strength in You. You are my Father, and I will place my hope, my trust, and my faith in You. Amen

for guys

What Kind of Example?

Stay at your post reading Scripture, giving counsel, teaching. And that special gift of ministry you were given when the leaders of the church laid hands on you and prayed—keep that dusted off and in use. Cultivate these things. Immerse yourself in them. The people will all see you mature right before their eyes! Keep a firm grasp on both your character and your teaching. Don't be diverted. Just keep at it. Both you and those who hear you will experience salvation.

1 TIMOTHY 4:13-16 MSG

Okay, here's a question: What kind of example are you? Are you the kind of guy whose life serves as a powerful example of decency and morality? Are you a guy whose behavior serves as a positive role model for others? Are you the kind of guy whose actions, day in and day out, are based upon integrity, fidelity, and a love for the Lord? If so, you are not only blessed by God, you are also a powerful force for good in a world that desperately needs positive influences such as yours.

Phillips Brooks advised, "Be such a man, and live such a life, that if every man were such as you, and every life a life like yours, this earth would be God's Paradise." And that's sound advice because our families and friends are watching . . . and so, for that matter, is God.

more stuff to think about

In our faith we follow in someone's steps.
In our faith we leave footprints to guide others.
It's the principle of discipleship.

MAX LUCADO

A holy life will produce the deepest impression.
Lighthouses blow no horns; they only shine.

D. L. MOODY

Today's Prayer

Lord, make me a worthy example to my family and friends. And, let my words and my deeds serve as a testimony to the changes You have made in my life. Let me praise You, Father, by following in the footsteps of Your Son, and let others see Him through me. Amen

for guys

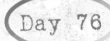

Kindness Is a Choice

Kind people do themselves a favor, but cruel people bring trouble on themselves.
PROVERBS 11:17 NCV

Kindness is a choice. Sometimes, when we feel happy or generous, we find it easy to be kind. Other times, when we are discouraged or tired, we can scarcely summon the energy to utter a single kind word. But, God's commandment is clear: He intends that we make the conscious choice to treat others with kindness and respect, no matter our circumstances, no matter our emotions.

In the busyness and confusion of daily life, it is easy to lose focus, and it is easy to become frustrated. We are imperfect human beings struggling to manage our lives as best we can, but we often fall short. When we are distracted or disappointed, we may neglect to share a kind word or a kind deed. This oversight hurts others, but it hurts us most of all.

Today, slow yourself down and be alert for people who need your smile, your kind words, or your helping hand. Make kindness a centerpiece of your dealings with others. They will be blessed, and you will be too.

2 MINUTES A DAY

more stuff to think about

When you extend hospitality to others, you're not trying to
impress people, you're trying to reflect God to them.

MAX LUCADO

Be so preoccupied with good will that
you haven't room for ill will.

E. STANLEY JONES

Today's Prayer

Help me, Lord, to see the needs of those around me.
Today, let me show courtesy to those who cross my path.
Today, let me spread kind words in honor of Your Son.
Today, let forgiveness rule my heart. And every day,
Lord, let my love for Christ be demonstrated through
the acts of kindness that I offer to those who need the
healing touch of the Master's hand. Amen

for guys

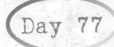

A Little Silence

Be silent before the Lord and wait expectantly for Him.
PSALM 37:7 HCSB

When you have doubts, remember this: God isn't on a coffee break, and He hasn't moved out of town. God isn't taking a long vacation, and He isn't snoozing on the couch. He's right here, right now, listening to your thoughts and prayers, watching over your every move.

The Bible teaches that a wonderful way to get to know God is simply to be still and listen to Him. But sometimes, you may find it hard to slow down and listen. As the demands of everyday life weigh down upon you, you may be tempted to ignore God's presence or—worse yet—to rebel against His commandments. But, when you quiet yourself and acknowledge His presence, God touches your heart and restores your spirits. So why not let Him do it right now? If you really want to know Him better, silence is a wonderful place to start.

more stuff to think about

Growth takes place in quietness, in hidden ways,
in silence and solitude.
The process is not accessible to observation.

EUGENE PETERSON

Silence is as fit a garment for devotion as
any other language.

C. H. SPURGEON

Today's Prayer

Dear Lord, in the quiet moments of this day, I will turn
my thoughts and prayers to You. In silence, I will sense
Your presence, and I will seek Your will for my life,
knowing that when I accept Your peace, I will be blessed
today and throughout eternity. Amen

for guys

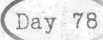

Tackling Tough Times

God is our refuge and strength, always ready to help in times of trouble. So we will not fear, even if earthquakes come and mountains crumble to the sea.

PSALM 46:1-2 NLT

From time to time, all of us have to face troubles and disappointments. When we do, God stands ready to protect us. Psalm 147 promises, "He heals the brokenhearted and bandages their wounds" (v. 3, NCV), but it doesn't say that He heals them instantly. Usually, it takes time for God to heal His children.

If you find yourself in any kind of trouble, pray about it and ask God for help. And then be patient. God will work things out, just as He has promised, but He will do it in His own time and according to His own plan.

more stuff to think about

Jesus does not say, "There is no storm."
He says, "I am here, do not toss, but trust."

VANCE HAVNER

Your greatest ministry will likely come out of
your greatest hurt.

RICK WARREN

Today's Prayer

Lord, sometimes life is so difficult that I can't see any
hope for the future. But with You, there is always hope.
Keep me mindful that there is nothing that will happen
today that You and I can't handle together. Amen

for guys

The Right Crowd

Love from the center of who you are; don't fake it.
Run for dear life from evil; hold on for dear life to good.
Be good friends who love deeply;
practice playing second fiddle.
ROMANS 12:9-10 MSG

Are you hanging out with people who make you a better Christian, or are you spending time with people who encourage you to stray from your faith? The answer to this question will have a surprising impact on the condition of your spiritual health. Why? Because peer pressure is very real and very powerful. That's why one of the best ways to ensure that you follow Christ is to find fellow believers who are willing to follow Him with you.

Many elements of society seek to mold us into more worldly beings; God, on the other hand, seeks to mold us into new beings, new creations through Christ, beings that are most certainly not conformed to this world. If we are to please God, we must resist the pressures that society seeks to impose upon us, and we must conform ourselves, instead, to His will, to His path, and to His Son.

more stuff to think about

A friend who loves will be more concerned about what is best for you than being accepted by you.

CHARLES STANLEY

A friend is one who makes me do my best.

OSWALD CHAMBERS

Today's Prayer

Thank You Lord, for my friends, the people who enrich my life. I pray for them today, and ask Your blessings upon them . . . and upon me. Amen

for guys

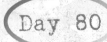

Every Day with God

*Morning by morning he wakens me and opens my
understanding to his will. The Sovereign Lord
has spoken to me, and I have listened.*

Isaiah 50:4-5 NLT

Daily life is a tapestry of habits, and no habit is more important to your spiritual health than the discipline of daily prayer and devotion to the Creator. When you begin each day with your head bowed and your heart lifted, you are reminded of God's love and God's laws.

Each day has 1,440 minutes—do you value your relationship with God enough to spend a few of those minutes with Him? He deserves that much of your time and more. But if you find that you're simply "too busy" for a daily chat with your Father in heaven, it's time to take a long, hard look at your priorities and your values.

If you've acquired the unfortunate habit of trying to "squeeze" God into the corners of your life, it's time to reshuffle the items on your to-do list by placing God first. God wants your undivided attention, not the leftovers of your day. So, if you haven't already done so, form the habit of spending quality time with your Creator. He deserves it . . . and so, for that matter, do you.

more stuff to think about

I suggest you discipline yourself to spend time daily in
a systematic reading of God's Word. Make this "quiet time"
a priority that nobody can change.

WARREN WIERSBE

We must appropriate the tender mercy of God every day
after conversion or problems quickly develop.
We need His grace daily in order to live a righteous life.

JIM CYMBALA

Today's Prayer

Lord, help me to hear Your direction for my life in the
quiet moments when I study Your Holy Word. And as
I go about my daily activities, let everything that I say
and do be pleasing to You. Amen

for guys

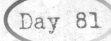

Too Much Stuff?

*Do not store up for yourselves treasures on earth, where
moth and rust destroy, and where thieves break in and steal.
But store up for yourselves treasures in heaven,
where moth and rust do not destroy, and where thieves do
not break in and steal. For where your treasure is,
there your heart will be also.*

Matthew 6:19-21 NIV

Are you a guy who's overly concerned with the stuff
that money can buy? Hopefully not. On the grand
stage of a well-lived life, material possessions
should play a rather small role. Of course, we all need the
basic necessities of life, but once we meet those needs for
ourselves and for our families, the piling up of possessions
creates more problems than it solves. Our real riches, of
course, are not of this world. We are never really rich until
we are rich in spirit.

Our society is in love with money and the things that
money can buy. God is not. God cares about people, not
possessions, and so must we. We must, to the best of our
abilities, love our neighbors as ourselves, and we must, to
the best of our abilities, resist the mighty temptation to place
possessions ahead of people.

Money, in and of itself, is not evil; worshipping money is.
So today, as you prioritize matters of importance in your life,
remember that God is almighty, but the dollar is not.

more stuff to think about

He is no fool who gives what he cannot keep to gain
what he cannot lose.

JIM ELLIOT

When possessions become our god, we become
materialistic and greedy . . .
and we forfeit our contentment and our joy.

CHARLES SWINDOLL

Today's Prayer

Lord, my greatest possession is my relationship with
You through Jesus Christ. You have promised that, when
I first seek Your kingdom and Your righteousness,
You will give me whatever I need. Let me trust You
completely, Lord, for my needs, both material and
spiritual, this day and always. Amen

for guys

Who Will You Follow?

"Follow Me," Jesus told them, "and I will make you into fishers of men!" Immediately they left their nets and followed Him.

MARK 1:17-18 HCSB

Can you honestly say that you're passionate about your faith and that you're really following Jesus? Hopefully so. But if you're preoccupied with other things—or if you're strictly a one-day-a-week Christian—then you're in need of a major-league spiritual makeover.

Jesus doesn't want you to be a lukewarm believer; Jesus wants you to be a "new creation" through Him. And that's exactly what you should want for yourself, too. Nothing is more important than your wholehearted commitment to your Creator and to His only begotten Son. Your faith must never be an afterthought; it must be your ultimate priority, your ultimate possession, and your ultimate passion.

You are the recipient of Christ's love. Accept it enthusiastically and share it passionately. Jesus deserves your undivided attention. And when you give it to Him, you'll be forever grateful that you did.

more stuff to think about

Christ is like a river that is continually flowing. There are always fresh supplies of water coming from the fountain-head, so that a man may live by it and be supplied with water all his life. So Christ is an ever-flowing fountain; he is continually supplying His people, and the fountain is not spent. They who live upon Christ may have fresh supplies from Him for all eternity; they may have an increase of blessedness that is new, and new still, and which never will come to an end.

JONATHAN EDWARDS

Imagine the spiritual strength the disciples drew from walking hundreds of miles with Jesus . . . 3 John 4.

JOHN MAXWELL

Today's Prayer

Dear Lord, You sent Jesus to save the world and to save me. I thank You for Jesus, and I will do my best to follow Him, today and forever. Amen

for guys

Time for a Celebration!

David and the whole house of Israel were celebrating with all their might before the LORD, with songs and with harps, lyres, tambourines, sistrums and cymbals.

2 Samuel 6:5 NIV

D o you feel like celebrating? If you're a believer, you should! When you allow Christ to reign over your heart, today and every day should be a time for joyful celebration.

What do you expect from the day ahead? Are you expecting God to do wonderful things, or are you living beneath a cloud of worry and doubt? The words of Psalm 118:24 remind us that every day is a gift from God. So whatever this day holds for you, begin it and end it with God as your partner and Christ as your Savior. And throughout the day, give thanks to the One who created you and saved you. God's love for you is infinite. Accept it; celebrate it; and be thankful.

2 minutes A DAY

more stuff to think about

Joy is the great note all throughout the Bible.

OSWALD CHAMBERS

Some of us seem so anxious about avoiding hell that we
forget to celebrate our journey toward heaven.

PHILIP YANCEY

Today's Prayer

Dear Lord, You have given me so many reasons
to celebrate. Today, let me choose an attitude of
cheerfulness. Let me be a joyful Christian, Lord, quick
to laugh and slow to anger. Let me praise You, Lord,
and give thanks for Your blessings. Today is Your
creation; let me celebrate it...and You. Amen

for guys

Radical Optimism

I can do everything through him that gives me strength.
PHILIPPIANS 4:13 NIV

Are you a radically optimistic believer? Do you believe that God has a wonderful plan that is perfectly suited for your life? And do you believe that when your life here on earth is done, you will enjoy the priceless gift of eternal life? Hopefully so, because Christianity and pessimism don't mix. Why? Because Christians have every reason to be optimistic about life here on earth and life eternal.

Today, make this promise to yourself and keep it: vow to be a hope-filled Christian. Think optimistically about your life and your future. Trust your hopes, not your fears. Take time to celebrate God's glorious creation. And then, when you've filled your heart with hope and gladness, share your optimism with your friends. They'll be better for it, and so will you. But not necessarily in that order.

more stuff to think about

Christ can put a spring in your step and a thrill in your heart.
Optimism and cheerfulness are products of knowing Christ.

BILLY GRAHAM

The popular idea of faith is of a certain obstinate optimism:
the hope, tenaciously held in the face of trouble,
that the universe is fundamentally friendly
and things may get better.

J. I. PACKER

Today's Prayer

Lord, You care for me, You love me, and You have given
me the priceless gift of eternal life through Your Son
Jesus. Because of You, Lord, I have every reason to live
each day with celebration and hope. Help me to face
this day with a spirit of optimism and thanksgiving
so that I may lift the spirits of those I meet as I share
the Good News of Your Son. And, let me focus my
thoughts on You and Your incomparable gifts today
and forever. Amen

for guys

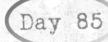

Beyond Mistakes

*Instead, God has chosen the world's foolish things
to shame the wise, and God has chosen the world's weak
things to shame the strong.*

1 CORINTHIANS 1:27 HCSB

Mistakes: nobody likes 'em but everybody makes 'em. Sometimes, even if you're a very good person, you're going to mess things up. And when you do, God is always ready to forgive you—He'll do His part, but you should be willing to do your part, too. Here's what you need to do:

1. If you've been engaging in behavior that is against the will of God, cease and desist (that means stop). 2. If you made a mistake, learn from it and don't repeat it (that's called getting smarter). 3. If you've hurt somebody, apologize and ask for forgiveness (that's called doing the right thing). 4. Ask for God's forgiveness, too (He'll give it whenever you ask, but you do need to ask!).

Mistakes are the price you pay for being human; repeated mistakes are the price you pay for being stubborn. So don't be hardheaded: learn from your experiences—the first time!

more stuff to think about

I hope you don't mind me telling you all this.
One can learn only by seeing one's mistakes.

C. S. LEWIS

Truth will sooner come out of error than from confusion.

FRANCIS BACON

Today's Prayer

Dear Lord, there's a right way to do things and a wrong
way to do things. When I do things that are wrong,
help me be quick to ask for forgiveness . . . and quick
to correct my mistakes. Amen

for guys

Finding Hope

*This hope we have as an anchor of the soul,
a hope both sure and steadfast.*

HEBREWS 6:19 NASB

There are few sadder sights on earth than the sight of a girl or guy who has lost hope. In difficult times, hope can be elusive, but those who place their faith in God's promises need never lose it. After all, God is good; His love endures; He has promised His children the gift of eternal life. And, God keeps his promises.

If you find yourself falling into the spiritual traps of worry and discouragement, seek the healing touch of Jesus and the encouraging words of fellow believers. And if you find a friend in need, remind him or her of the peace that is found through a genuine relationship with Christ. It was Christ who promised, "I have told you these things so that in Me you may have peace. In the world you have suffering. But take courage! I have conquered the world." (John 16:33 HCSB). This world can be a place of trials and troubles, but as believers, we are secure. God has promised us peace, joy, and eternal life. And, of course, God keeps His promises today, tomorrow, and forever.

more stuff to think about

If your hopes are being disappointed just now,
it means that they are being purified.

OSWALD CHAMBERS

Faith looks back and draws courage;
hope looks ahead and keeps desire alive.

JOHN ELDREDGE

Today's Prayer

Today, Dear Lord, I will live in hope. If I become
discouraged, I will turn to You. If I grow weary, I will
seek strength in You. In every aspect of my life, I will
trust You. You are my Father, Lord, and I place my
hope and my faith in You. Amen

for guys

The Best Policy

Better to be poor and honest than a rich person no one can trust.
PROVERBS 19:1 MSG

It has been said on many occasions and in many ways that honesty is the best policy. For believers, it is far more important to note that honesty is God's policy. And if we are to be servants worthy of our Savior, Jesus Christ, we must be honest and forthright in our communications with others.

Sometimes, honesty is difficult; sometimes, honesty is painful; always, honesty is God's commandment. In the Book of Exodus, God did not command, "Thou shalt not bear false witness when it is convenient." And He didn't say, "Thou shalt not bear false witness most of the time." God said, "Thou shalt not bear false witness against thy neighbor." Period.

Sometime soon, perhaps even today, you will be tempted to bend the truth or perhaps even to break it. Resist that temptation. Truth is God's way...and it must also be yours. Period.

A little lie is like a little pregnancy.
It doesn't take long before everyone knows.

C. S. LEWIS

God doesn't expect you to be perfect,
but he does insist on complete honesty.

RICK WARREN

Today's Prayer

Heavenly Father, You instruct Your children to seek truth and to live righteously. Help me always to live according to Your commandments. Sometimes, Lord, speaking the truth is difficult, but let me always speak truthfully and forthrightly. And, let me walk righteously and courageously so that others might see Your Grace reflected in my words and my deeds. Amen

Healthy Habits

Do not be deceived: "Evil company corrupts good habits."
1 CORINTHIANS 15:33 NKJV

It's an old saying and a true one: First, you make your habits, and then your habits make you. Some habits will inevitably bring you closer to God; other habits will lead you away from the path He has chosen for you. If you sincerely desire to improve your spiritual health, you must honestly examine the habits that make up the fabric of your day. And you must abandon those habits that are displeasing to God.

If you trust God, and if you keep asking for His help, He can transform your life. If you sincerely ask Him to help you, the same God who created the universe will help you defeat the harmful habits that have heretofore defeated you. So, if at first you don't succeed, keep praying. God is listening, and He's ready to help you become a better person if you ask Him . . . so ask today.

more stuff to think about

Since behaviors become habits,
make them work with you and not against you.

E. STANLEY JONES

You will never change your life until you change
something you do daily.

JOHN MAXWELL

Today's Prayer

Dear Lord, help me break bad habits and form good
ones. And let my actions be pleasing to You, today and
every day. Amen

for guys

Swing Away!

*Let us not become weary in doing good, for at the proper
time we will reap a harvest if we do not give up.*

GALATIANS 6:9 NIV

His adoring fans called him the "Sultan of Swat." He
was Babe Ruth, the baseball player who set records
for home runs and strikeouts. Babe's philosophy was
simple. He said, "Never let the fear of striking out get in your
way." That's smart advice on the diamond or off.

Of course it's never wise to take foolish risks (so buckle
up, slow down, and don't do anything stupid!). But when
it comes to the game of life, you should not let the fear of
failure keep you from taking your swings.

Today, ask God for the courage to step beyond the
boundaries of your self-doubts. Ask Him to guide you to
a place where you can realize your full potential—a place
where you are freed from the fear of failure. Ask Him to do
His part, and promise Him that you will do your part. Don't
ask Him to lead you to a "safe" place; ask Him to lead you
to the "right" place . . . and remember: those two places are
seldom the same.

more stuff to think about

If you learn from a defeat, you have not really lost.

ZIG ZIGLAR

Success or failure can be pretty well predicted by
the degree to which the heart is fully in it.

JOHN ELDREDGE

Today's Prayer

Dear Lord, even when I'm afraid of failure, give me the
courage to try. Remind me that with You by my side, I
really have nothing to fear. So today, Father, I will live
courageously as I place my faith in You. Amen

for guys

His Disciple

He has showed you, O man, what is good. And what does the LORD require of you? To act justly and to love mercy and to walk humbly with your God.

MICAH 6:8 NIV

When Jesus addressed His disciples, He warned that each one must, "take up his cross and follow me." The disciples must have known exactly what the Master meant. In Jesus' day, prisoners were forced to carry their own crosses to the location where they would be put to death. Thus, Christ's message was clear: in order to follow Him, Christ's disciples must deny themselves and, instead, trust Him completely. Nothing has changed since then.

If we are to be disciples of Christ, we must trust Him and place Him at very center of our beings. Jesus never comes "next." He is always first. The paradox, of course, is that only by sacrificing ourselves to Him do we gain salvation for ourselves.

Do you seek to be a worthy disciple of Christ? Then pick up His cross today and every day that you live. When you do, He will bless you now and forever.

more stuff to think about

A disciple is a follower of Christ. That means you take on His priorities as your own. His agenda becomes your agenda. His mission becomes your mission.

CHARLES STANLEY

There is not Christianity without a cross, for you cannot be a disciple of Jesus without taking up your cross.

HENRY BLACKABY

Today's Prayer

Help me, Lord, to understand what cross I am to bear this day. Give me the strength and the courage to carry that cross along the path of Your choosing so that I may be a worthy disciple of Your Son. Amen

for guys

Wisdom Now!

*Do you want to be counted wise, to build a reputation for
wisdom? Here's what you do: Live well, live wisely,
live humbly. It's the way you live,
not the way you talk, that counts.*

JAMES 3:13 MSG

Wisdom is not like a dandelion or a mushroom; it
does not spring up overnight. It is, instead, like
an oak tree that starts as a tiny acorn, grows into
a sapling, and eventually reaches up to the sky, tall and
strong. To become wise, you must seek God's wisdom and
live according to His Word. To become wise, you must seek
wisdom with consistency and purpose. To become wise, you
must not only learn the lessons of the Christian life, you must
also live by them.

Are you passionate in your pursuit of God's wisdom?
And do you sincerely seek to live a life of righteousness?
If so, you must study the ultimate source of wisdom: the
Word of God. You must seek out worthy teachers and listen
carefully to their advice. You must associate, day in and day
out, with godly friends. And, you must act in accordance
with your beliefs. When you do these things, you will become
wise . . . and you will be a blessing to your friends, to your
family, and to the world.

more stuff to think about

If you lack knowledge, go to school.
If you lack wisdom, get on your knees.

VANCE HAVNER

The more wisdom enters our hearts, the more we will
be able to trust our hearts in difficult situations.

JOHN ELDREDGE

Today's Prayer

Dear Lord, when I trust in the wisdom of the world, I am often led astray, but when I trust in Your wisdom, I build my life upon a firm foundation. Today and every day, I will trust Your Word and follow it, knowing that the ultimate wisdom is Your wisdom, and the ultimate truth is Your truth. Amen

for guys

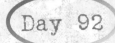
God's Guidance

Every morning he wakes me. He teaches me to listen like a student. The Lord God helps me learn...
IsaiaH 50:4-5 NCV

The Bible promises that God will guide you if you let Him. Your job, of course, is to let Him. But sometimes, you will be tempted to do otherwise. Sometimes, you'll be tempted to go along with the crowd; other times, you'll be tempted to do things your way, not God's way. When you feel those temptations, resist them.

What will you allow to guide you through the coming day: your own desires (or, for that matter, the desires of your friends)? Or will you allow God to lead the way? The answer should be obvious. You should let God be your guide. When you entrust your life to Him completely and without reservation, God will give you the strength to meet any challenge, the courage to face any trial, and the wisdom to live in His righteousness. So trust Him today and seek His guidance. When you do, your next step will be the right one.

more stuff to think about

We must always invite Jesus to be the navigator of our plans,
desires, wills, and emotions, for He is the way,
the truth, and the life.

BILL BRIGHT

God's plan for our guidance is for us to grow gradually in
wisdom before we get to the crossroads.

BILL HYBELS

Today's Prayer

Dear Lord, Thank You for Your constant presence and
Your constant love. I draw near to You this day with
the confidence that You are ready to guide me. Help me
walk closely with You, Father, and help me share Your
Good News with all who cross my path. Amen

for guys

Getting It Done Now

If you make a promise to God, don't be slow to keep it.
God is not happy with fools,
so give God what you promised.

ECCLESIASTES 5:4 NCV

When something important needs to be done, the best time to do it is sooner rather than later. But sometimes, instead of doing the smart thing (which, by the way, is choosing "sooner"), we may choose "later." When we do, we may pay a heavy price for our shortsightedness.

Are you one of those people who puts things off till the last minute? If so, it's time to change you ways. Your procrastination is probably the result of your shortsighted attempt to postpone (or avoid altogether) the discomfort that you associate with a particular activity. Get over it!

Whatever "it" is, do it now. When you do, you won't have to worry about "it" later.

more stuff to think about

Now is the only time worth having because,
indeed, it is the only time we have.

C. H. SPURGEON

Do noble things, do not dream them all day long.

CHARLES KINGSLEY

Today's Prayer

Dear Lord, today is a new day. Help me tackle the important tasks immediately, even if those tasks are unpleasant. Don't let me put off until tomorrow what I should do today. Amen

for guys

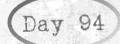
The Dating Game

Do not be unequally yoked together with unbelievers.
For what fellowship has righteousness with lawlessness?
And what communion has light with darkness?

2 CORINTHIANS 6:14 NKJV

O h, how glorious are the dreams of love—but oh how tough it is to turn those dreams into reality! If you're still searching for Miss Right, be patient, be prudent, and be picky. Look for a girl whose values you respect, whose behavior you approve of, and whose faith you admire. Remember that appearances can be deceiving and tempting, so watch your step. And when it comes to the important task of building a lifetime relationship with the girl of your dreams, pray about it! God is waiting to give His approval—or not—but He won't give it until He's asked. So ask, listen, and decide accordingly.

more stuff to think about

Be faithful in the little practices of love which will build in
you the life of holiness and will make you Christlike.

MOTHER TERESA

We discover our role in life through
our relationships with others.

RICK WARREN

Today's Prayer

Lord, I will let You rule over every aspect of my life,
including my relationships. And I know that when I
do, You will help me make choices that are right for me,
today and every day that I live. Amen

for guys

When You Have Doubts

Such doubters are thinking two different things at the same time, and they cannot decide about anything they do. They should not think they will receive anything from the Lord.

JAMES 1:8 NCV

If you've never had any doubts about your faith, then you can stop reading this page now and skip to the next. But if you've ever been plagued by doubts about your faith or your God, keep reading.

Even some of the most faithful Christians are, at times, beset by occasional bouts of discouragement and doubt. But even when we feel far removed from God, God is never far removed from us. He is always with us, always willing to calm the storms of life—always willing to replace our doubts with comfort and assurance.

Whenever you're plagued by doubts, that's precisely the moment you should seek God's presence by genuinely seeking to establish a deeper, more meaningful relationship with His Son. Then you may rest assured that in time, God will calm your fears, answer your prayers, and restore your confidence.

more stuff to think about

We basically have two choices to make in dealing
with the mysteries of God. We can wrestle
with Him or we can rest in Him.

CALVIN MILLER

Doubt may not always be a sign that a man is wrong;
it may be a sign that he is thinking.

OSWALD CHAMBERS

Today's Prayer

Dear God, sometimes this world can be a puzzling
place, filled with uncertainty and doubt. When I am
unsure of my next step, keep me mindful that You are
always near and that You can overcome any challenge.
Give me faith, Father, and let me remember always that
with Your love and Your power, I can live courageously
and faithfully today and every day. Amen

for guys

Love According to God

*This is my command: Love one another the way
I loved you. This is the very best way to love.
Put your life on the line for your friends.*

JOHN 15:12-13 MSG

Love, like everything else in this wonderful world, begins and ends with God, but the middle part belongs to us. During the brief time that we have here on earth, God has given each of us the opportunity to become a loving person—or not. God has given each of us the opportunity to be kind, to be courteous, to be cooperative, and to be forgiving—or not. God has given each of us the chance to obey the Golden Rule, or to make up our own rules as we go. If we obey God's rules, we're safe, but if we do otherwise, we're headed for trouble in a hurry.

Building lasting relationships requires compassion, wisdom, empathy, kindness, courtesy, and forgiveness. If that sounds a lot like work, it is—which is perfectly fine with God. Why? Because He knows that you are capable of doing that work, and because He knows that the fruits of your labors will enrich the lives of your loved ones and the lives of generations yet unborn.

more stuff to think about

How do you spell love? When you reach the point where the happiness, security, and development of another person is as much of a driving force to you as your own happiness, security, and development, then you have a mature love. True love is spelled G-I-V-E. It is not based on what you can get, but rooted in what you can give to the other person.

JOSH MCDOWELL

Love is not grabbing, or self-centered, or selfish. Real love is being able to contribute to the happiness of another person without expecting to get anything in return.

JAMES DOBSON

Today's Prayer

Lord, You have given me the gift of eternal love; let me share that gift with the world. Help me, Father, to show kindness to those who cross my path, and let me show tenderness and unfailing love to my family and friends. Make me generous with words of encouragement and praise. And, help me always to reflect the love that Christ Jesus gave me so that through me, others might find Him. Amen

for guys

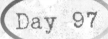

The Gift of Eternal Life

Just then someone came up and asked Him, "Teacher, what good must I do to have eternal life?" "Why do you ask Me about what is good?" He said to him. "There is only One who is good. If you want to enter into life, keep the commandments."

MATTHEW 19:16-17 HCSB

Your ability to envision the future, like your life here on earth, is limited. God's vision, however, is not burdened by any such limitations. He sees all things, He knows all things, and His plans for you endure for all time.

God's plans are not limited to the events of life-here-on-earth. Your Heavenly Father has bigger things in mind for you . . . much bigger things. So praise the Creator for the gift of eternal life and share the Good News with all who cross your path. You have given your heart to the Son, so you belong to the Father—today, tomorrow, and for all eternity.

more stuff to think about

Teach us to set our hopes on heaven, to hold firmly to
the promise of eternal life, so that we can withstand
the struggles and storms of this world.

MAX LUCADO

God loves you and wants you to experience peace
and life—abundant and eternal.

BILLY GRAHAM

Today's Prayer

Lord, I am only here on this earth for a brief while. But,
You have offered me the priceless gift of eternal life
through Your Son Jesus. I accept Your gift, Lord, with
thanksgiving and praise. Let me share the good news of
my salvation with those who need Your healing touch.
Amen

for guys

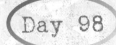

Richly Blessed

The Lord bless you and keep you; The Lord make His face
shine upon you, And be gracious to you.
NUMBERS 6:24-25 NKJV

Have you counted your blessings lately? If you sincerely wish to follow in Christ's footsteps, you should make thanksgiving a habit, a regular part of your daily routine.

How has God blessed you? First and foremost, He has given you the gift of eternal life through the sacrifice of His only begotten Son, but the blessings don't stop there. Today, take time to make a partial list of the God's gifts to you: the talents, the opportunities, the possessions, and the relationships that you may, on occasion, take for granted. And then, when you've spent sufficient time listing your blessings, offer a prayer of gratitude to the Giver of all things good . . . and, to the best of your ability, use your gifts for the glory of His kingdom.

more stuff to think about

It is when we give ourselves to be a blessing that we can
specially count on the blessing of God.

ANDREW MURRAY

We prevent God from giving us the great spiritual gifts
He has in store for us, because we do not
give thanks for daily gifts.

DIETRICH BONHOEFFER

Today's Prayer

Today, Lord, let me count my blessings with
thanksgiving in my heart. You have cared for me,
Lord, and I will give You the glory and the praise. Let
me accept Your blessings and Your gifts, and let me
share them with others, just as You first shared them
with me. Amen

for guys

God's Timetable

He has made everything beautiful in its time. He has also set eternity in the hearts of men; yet they cannot fathom what God has done from beginning to end.

ECCLESIASTES 3:11 NIV

Are you anxious for God to work out His plan for your life? Who isn't? As believers, we all want God to do great things for us and through us, and we want Him to do those things now. But sometimes, God has other plans. Sometimes, God's timetable does no coincide with our own. It's worth noting, however, that God's timetable is always perfect.

The next time you find your patience tested to the limit, remember that the world unfolds according to God's plan, not ours. Sometimes, we must wait patiently, and that's as it should be. After all, think how patient God has been with us.

more stuff to think about

Will not the Lord's time be better than your time?

C. H. SPURGEON

God has a designated time when his promise will be fulfilled and the prayer will be answered.

JIM CYMBALA

Today's Prayer

Dear Lord, Your wisdom is infinite, and the timing of Your Heavenly plan is perfect. You have a plan for my life that is grander than I can imagine. When I am impatient, remind me that You are never early or late. You are always on time, Father, so let me trust in You. Amen

for guys

How Much Love?

His banner over me was love.

SONG OF SOLOMON 2:4 KJV

How much does God love you? As long as you're alive, you'll never be able to figure it out because God's love is just too big to comprehend. But this much we know: God loves you so much that He sent His Son Jesus to come to this earth and to die for you! And, when you accepted Jesus into your heart, God gave you a gift that is more precious than gold: the gift of eternal life.

God's love is bigger and more powerful than anybody can imagine, but His love is very real. So do yourself a favor right now: accept God's love with open arms and welcome His Son Jesus into your heart. When you do, your life will be changed today, tomorrow, and forever.

more stuff to think about

God wants to emancipate his people; he wants to set them free. He wants his people to be not slaves but sons. He wants them governed not by law but by love.

MAX LUCADO

The hope we have in Jesus is the anchor for the soul—something sure and steadfast, preventing drifting or giving way, lowered to the depth of God's love.

FRANKLIN GRAHAM

Today's Prayer

Dear Lord, the Bible tells me that You are my loving Father. I thank You, Lord, for Your love and for Your Son. Amen

for guys